"The Bible repeatedly co[...] strangers' on earth whos[...] struggle to keep Christ at the center of our identity. Mabel Ninan's beautifully written *Far from Home* serves as a guide to rediscovering our core identity in Christ. It's a message the church desperately needs."

—**Matthew Soerens**
US director of church mobilization and advocacy, World Relief, and coauthor of *Welcoming the Stranger* and *Seeking Refuge*

"Mabel gives us her vibrant, challenging, and uplifting personal journey as an immigrant in a foreign land. This book will enlighten the Christian of their personal identity in Christ and show that our true home resides with our Father in heaven."

—**Dr. Bryan Loritts**
author of *Insider/Outsider*

"'I am an immigrant.' Mabel Ninan begins *Far from Home* with this simple yet profound declaration. With a heart ready to serve, eager to connect through genuine fellowship, and willing to see the world as a citizen of heaven, this reader responded, 'Me too!'"

—**Xochitl Dixon**
writer for *Our Daily Bread* and author of *Different Like Me* and *Waiting for God*

"*Far from Home* is for every person who's longed to put down roots. Through the author's immigrant journey, we learn to make our home with God wherever we happen to live."

—**Monica Schmelter**
host of Christian Television Network's *Bridges* and coauthor of the *Messy to Meaningful* books

"By sensitively sharing her heart about her identity struggles as an immigrant, Mabel does more than draw out our empathy. She sets us up to understand our own immigrant status as Christians on this planet. Come away from this amazing work with your priorities in their proper place, knowing more assuredly than ever that heaven is your real home."

—**Dr. Sharon Norris Elliott**
founder/CEO of AuthorizeMe Literary Agency, Life That Matters Ministries, and Milk & Honey Life Retreats

"As Christ followers, we are all sojourners longing for our heavenly home. Whether you have experienced long-term global exposure or never left your home state, you will enjoy and grow from Mabel's candid description of her intentional-yet-unexpected cultural journey, her heart through it, and most of all, the God behind her spiritual depth."

—**Stephanie Rousselle**
founder of *Gospel Spice* Ministries and
host of the podcast Gospel Spice

"Being myself an immigrant to the US, far from family and the familiar, and having resided in several strange abodes, I found *Far from Home* riddled with 'me too' moments. An inspiring read, especially to those far from home and those experiencing homelessness physically, emotionally, or spiritually."

—**Ifueko Fex Ogbomo**
prize-winning poet and storyteller, Nigerian immigrant, and author
of *Yellow Eyes Gone White!*

"Beautifully transparent, Mabel Ninan shares her personal insight from a unique experience of immigration. Inside the stories of uprooted people, we discover the heart of God. This book is a beautiful reminder of our citizenship in His kingdom."

—**Christine Abraham**
founder and executive director, Bible Café Ministries

"In *Far from Home*, Mabel Ninan uses her own story as a foreigner in many unfamiliar places to remind all of us who feel 'stuck between two worlds' that our citizenship and identity are not ultimately rooted in a place but in a person. As we seek a city that is to come, we will all feel homesick, but Mabel reminds us that God is at work in us and through us wherever we are."

—**Gary Anderson**
lead pastor, Abundant Life Christian Fellowship,
Mountain View, CA

Far *from* Home

Discovering Your Identity as Foreigners on Earth

MABEL NINAN

IRON
STREAM
HARAMBEE
PRESS
Birmingham, Alabama

Far from Home

Iron Stream Harambee Press
An imprint of Iron Stream Media
100 Missionary Ridge
Birmingham, AL 35242
IronStreamMedia.com

Copyright © 2022 by Shwetha Mabel Maddela

No part of this publication may be reproduced, stored in a retrieval system, or transmitted in any form or by any means—electronic, mechanical, photocopying, recording, or otherwise—without the prior written permission of the publisher.

Iron Stream Media serves its authors as they express their views, which may not express the views of the publisher. While all the stories in this book are true, some of the details and names have been changed or deleted to protect the storyteller's identity. All stories are used by permission.

Library of Congress Control Number: 2022932498

All Scripture quotations, unless otherwise indicated, are taken from the Holy Bible, New International Version®, NIV®. Copyright ©1973, 1978, 1984, 2011 by Biblica, Inc.™ Used by permission of Zondervan. All rights reserved worldwide. www.zondervan.com The "NIV" and "New International Version" are trademarks registered in the United States Patent and Trademark Office by Biblica, Inc.™

Scripture quotation marked ESV is from the ESV® Bible (The Holy Bible, English Standard Version®), Copyright © 2001 by Crossway, a publishing ministry of Good News Publishers. Used by permission. All rights reserved.

Scripture quotations marked KJV are from The Authorized (King James) Version. Rights in the Authorized Version in the United Kingdom are vested in the Crown. Reproduced by permission of the Crown's patentee, Cambridge University Press

Scripture quotations marked NKJV taken from the New King James Version®. Copyright © 1982 by Thomas Nelson. Used by permission. All rights reserved.

Cover design by Hannah Linder Designs

ISBN: 978-1-64526-366-1 (paperback)
ISBN: 978-1-64526-367-8 (e-book)

1 2 3 4 5—26 25 24 23 22

I dedicate this book to my parents, Samson and Mallika.
I am who I am because of your love and sacrifice.

CONTENTS

Acknowledgments ix

Introduction xiii

Section One: Identity

Chapter 1   Change and Identity 1

Chapter 2   The Skein of Identity 13

Chapter 3   God Shapes Identity 25

Chapter 4   Citizenship in Heaven 35

Chapter 5   Identity and Calling 47

Chapter 6   Strangers on Earth 59

Section Two: Home

Chapter 7   Homeless on Earth 73

Chapter 8   Homesick for Heaven. 87

Chapter 9   Homeward Bound 101

Section Three: Community

Chapter 10   Craving for Community 115

Chapter 11   Unity in Diversity 129

Conclusion   Moving Forward 143

Appendix 1   Love Your Immigrant Neighbor:
Action Plan for Individuals 155

Appendix 2   Love Your Immigrant Neighbor:
Action Plan for Churches. 157

Appendix 3   Immigrant Heroes of the Bible 159

Appendix 4   Bible References on Heavenly Rewards 163

Appendix 5   Recommended Reading 167

About the Author 169

ACKNOWLEDGMENTS

For giving me abundant and eternal life, for making me an immigrant and a writer, for being my permanent home and anchor, I'm grateful to Jesus, my Lord and Savior. I owe my life to You.

Words cannot express how grateful I am to my parents who taught me everything about life, love, and God. They are my biggest cheerleaders, always encouraging me to follow my dreams and reminding me to put God first in my life.

I thank my sister, Joy, who never stops saying to me, "You are a good writer." During our single days, we spent hours in our bedroom talking about Christian books and how they impacted us. Little did we know that one of us would go on to write a book!

God has blessed me with an army of prayer warriors in India—my aunts, uncles, cousins, nephews, nieces, and in-laws. Though we are thousands of miles apart, I draw strength from their generous encouragement and love.

I'm grateful to my home churches in Hyderabad, India—Centenary Methodist English Church and New Life Assemblies of God Church—whose Sunday school teachers, youth leaders, pastors, and members poured into my life and laid a strong foundation for my faith. Friends from Methodist Youth Fellowship and Youth Alive continue to support my writing and speaking ministries.

The D'Costas and the Bhadrans opened their hearts and homes to us in Los Angeles when Simon and I were new to the US and became the Indian family we miss and crave. I'm grateful for their love, prayers, guidance, and support.

For *desi* fun and friendships and for cheering me on, I'm grateful to my friends from the South Bay Indian American Association in Los Angeles.

I thank the Kyles—Trey, Krys, Tim, and Kara—for showing God's love by adopting Simon, Ryan, and me into their family.

The women of Bible Study Fellowship in Torrance, California, helped me grow in my walk with God by sharing their lives with me and modeling faithfulness to me. I'm especially thankful to my former teaching leader, Sandy, for praying and encouraging me when I began writing this book.

Sincere thanks to the women of Bible Study Fellowship in San Jose, California, for their support and kindness. Thank you, Maria and Laura, for diligently praying for my writing ministry.

To all the South Asian families of our monthly Bible study group in San Jose, California, I'm deeply grateful. Huge thanks to Mohan, Sharmini, John uncle, and Kamali auntie for lifting me up with their words and prayers.

Thanks to John and Carol from Kontagious for showing me how to love immigrants with God's love.

I'm grateful to Gary Anderson, the pastor of my church, Abundant Life Christian Fellowship, and to the women of the Bible study group for their prayers and support.

This book would not have been made possible without two writers conferences that were instrumental in launching my career as an author, the Colorado Christian Writers Conference and the Mount Hermon Christian Writers Conference. I met authors, editors, agents, and other professionals who played an important role in moving my writing ministry forward. The workshops and mentoring clinics helped me hone my craft and learn about publishing and marketing books. I was impressed to see the comradery among authors and the passion with which they served God through writing. Special thanks to Cheri Cowell, Jan Kern, Erin Taylor Young, Cindy Lambert, and Kay Marshall Strom who took the time to teach, guide, and counsel me. I thank my friends whom I met at the conferences, Debbie Jones Warren, Danielle, Lesa Johnson, Stephanie Rousselle, Leigh Mackenzie, and Beverly Urbanic, for getting excited about my book and cheering me on.

Many thanks to my sisters from the Advanced Writers and Speakers Association for motivating me to keep Jesus at the center of my ministry. Thank you, Amber Weigand-Buckley, for your tremendous support. I'm also grateful to Monica Schmelter for her overwhelming kindness and encouragement.

For teaching me how to read and study God's Word, I'm thankful to the professors of Southern Baptist Theological Seminary.

Heartfelt thanks to my agent, Karen Neumair of Credo Communications, who had more confidence in me than I had in myself. I'm grateful for your discernment and guidance.

I owe a debt of gratitude to Edwina Perkins, the acquisitions editor of Harambee Press and Iron Stream Media, for taking a chance on me and championing my book. It is an honor and privilege to have my first book published by Harambee Press.

Larry J. Leech II, my editor, helped me polish the manuscript and put my best foot forward. His wise, gentle, and encouraging manner made editing enjoyable.

For the entire team at Harambee Press and Iron Stream Media, I'm sincerely grateful for taking me on and believing in this book.

When Xochitl Dixon told me that God put it on her heart to come alongside me and help me with my book, I was close to tears. She helped me write my book proposal and book, told me countless times that my writing was valuable, and stood by me when rejections piled on. She is not just my mentor but also a ministry partner, friend, and sister.

Ryan, my son, was only a little boy when God birthed this book in my heart. But in his own sweet ways, he has been supportive of my writing. He was hardly seven years of age when he prayed, "Dear God, help Mom write. Help her to believe that she is a good writer." I'm immensely grateful to God for choosing me as Ryan's mother.

My husband, my fellow sojourner and best friend, is the only witness, besides God, to my struggles and growth as an immigrant as well as a writer. I looked to him for comfort, strength, pep talks, and endless cups of chai. He helped me process my thoughts and give shape to the concepts of the book. With no family around, I depended solely on him to manage our son and the house during times when I had to devote my attention to writing. He is both my fiercest critic and most ardent fan. I thank God for Simon's love for me and his desire to see me flourish.

INTRODUCTION

I am an immigrant.

My story began in 2008 when my husband and I moved from India to the United States as newlyweds, excited about starting a new chapter in our lives. I felt confident, equipped, and ready for adventure.

About four months after landing on US soil, the excitement faded. Feelings of loneliness and loss engulfed me. With no family to lean on and no community to belong to, I felt cast adrift. I had to come to terms with living in an unfamiliar land. People looked different. Surroundings were strange. The language felt alien even though I grew up speaking English in India.

I had never lived in a place where I stood out. In my homeland, I was simply another brown, Indian girl. In America, however, I was an anomaly. This affected how I perceived myself. I also had to contend with the issue of anonymity. I had to start rebuilding my life from scratch because my slate had been erased clean. So clean that it wiped out my self-esteem and self-worth.

Because of my husband's job, we hopped from one place to another, never staying too long in one place to put down roots. California. India. New Jersey. India. New Jersey. India. Arkansas. India. California. Feelings of homelessness and homesickness became my companions. I longed for stability and permanence.

The transition from native to foreigner, from insider to outsider shook the foundation of my identity and faith. Born and raised in a Christian home in India, I arrived in the US as a thirty-year-old Christ follower, taught to rely on God through times of transition. Why, then, did the change disorient me? Why was Christ not enough for me? What was my purpose in life?

My struggles broke me down and brought me to my knees before the throne of God. I surrendered my questions and worries to Him. I saturated my mind with Scripture. I spent more time in His presence, desperate for solace and direction.

Intimacy with God refreshed my parched soul and restored joy in my life. The biggest transformation, however, was the renewing of my mind.

I gained a new perspective. I recognized the truth of what it meant to first be a citizen of heaven, regardless of where I had pitched my tent here on earth. I discovered how to find my identity, inextricably bound to Christ. I was a child of God before I was Indian or Indian American, I was loved and approved by Him. God confirmed that I was in fact, an immigrant in my very soul, a sojourner on earth. How could I really feel at home in this world, and how could any earthly home give me stability and security?

Embracing my biblical, immigrant identity changed everything.

Despair and discontent turned into joyful passion to serve God. I wanted to model Jesus, who came to the earth as a migrant, dedicated to fulfilling His God-ordained mission.

My immigrant identity gave me an eternal perspective, turning my eyes away from my circumstances and desires and fixing them on God's will for me. This new way of thinking inspired me to live for God, not myself. I realized the purpose of my earthly sojourn was to accomplish God's purposes.

Knowing my permanent home is with Jesus in heaven has brightened my days. His perfect and unchanging love for me fuels my homesickness. Thoughts of my promised inheritance and glorious future make hope bloom during dreary times. A better city awaits me. Better times are ahead.

If you are saved, you are a child of God and a stranger on earth: "Live out your time as foreigners here in reverent fear" (1 Peter 1:17). If you are a disciple of Jesus, you are not of this world: "They are not of the world, even as I am not of it" (John 17:16). And this earth is not our home. You are a citizen of heaven: "But our citizenship is in heaven. And we eagerly await a Savior from there, the Lord Jesus Christ" (Philippians 3:20).

While you read this book, I pray the gentle voice of the Holy Spirit will remind you of your eternal identity in Christ. You are loved and set apart by God to further His kingdom on earth. The Holy Spirit walks alongside you on your pilgrimage, as helper and guide, enabling you to participate in God's plans and glorify His name.

I hope these biblical truths instill in you an unquenchable thirst for fellowship with God and encourage you to chase after God's heart. I hope your eyes are opened to the limitless spiritual blessings that are yours as a citizen of God's kingdom. I hope you find comfort and strength to persevere in faith, looking ahead to that day when you will be united with God.

My desire also is the truth about our identity as foreigners will inspire us to transcend our differences and unite around our calling as Christians.

Far from Home is a practical guidebook to encourage and motivate you on your pilgrim journey, as you embrace a life that will not just survive but thrive as the curse of the temporal gives way to the promise of heaven.

In this book, I draw parallels between my experience as an Indian American immigrant and a spiritual immigrant to draw lessons about what it means to truly live as a citizen of heaven. To explain some of the biblical truths, I take a deeper look at the lives of the mighty patriarchs of our faith, Abraham, Isaac, Jacob, Joseph, and others who lived on the road, pitching their tents often in foreign cultures and countries.

I've structured this book around challenges that immigrants wrestle with the most, which broadly fall into three main categories: identity, home, and community. Each of these three sections is broken down into chapters. To help you internalize the message of this book and apply the learnings to your life, I have included reflection questions, action steps, and a prayer at the end of each chapter.

I wrote *Far from Home* so you will lean into your identity as a citizen of heaven, embrace your pilgrim journey on earth, and live with joy, meaning, and hope.

You, too, are an immigrant, just as I am.

Section One
Identity

CHAPTER 1
Change and Identity

But you remain the same, and your years will never end.

Psalm 102:27

January 2010. I opened my eyes on a typical wintery morning in New Jersey and fought back the dread while I watched my husband pack his laptop. Through the gap in the window blinds of our apartment in Jersey City, I saw the sky unpacking snow on everyone and everything below. People in the streets were on the move, walking and driving hurriedly, as though they could not wait to escape the snow.

My husband kissed me on the forehead and whispered goodbye before leaving for work. Simon looked fresh and happy, ready to take on another new day. I forced myself to smile back and waved him goodbye. Oblivious to the sorrow fermenting in my mind, he smiled at me when he shut the door behind him.

I closed my eyes and held my blanket closer. A wave of cold crept into my soul. I felt completely alone, not just in the apartment, but also in the city, in the country. No family. No friends. I sighed. No purpose.

Why should I wake up? Who is waiting for me? I drifted in and out of sleep.

Trapped in an unending cycle of loneliness and despair, I had nowhere to go.

But I traveled in my mind. I explored memories of a life I lived a few months, a few years ago, in a faraway land . . . India. A land of spices and religions, ancient customs and traditions, and hundreds of languages and cultures. My birthplace and home. Being there felt a lifetime ago.

My eyes still closed, I went back in time to my childhood in Hyderabad, a bustling city nestled in southern India. My sister and I had completed our homework for the day after returning from school and rushed outside to play hopscotch with other children from our neighborhood. An hour went by, maybe two, before Mom hollered at us to come back inside the house. It was dinner time. Sweaty, thirsty, and exhausted, Joy and I raced back home to devour the rice, *dal* (lentil soup), and potato dish that Mom had prepared.

Rooted in One Place

We were a comfortably settled and modest middle-class family. My dad worked as a bank teller during the day and moonlighted as a singer in the evenings and during weekends. My mother had been a stay-at-home mom until we were middle schoolers. Then, she went back to school, earned her master's degree in education, and became the principal of a school. Only about a year younger than I, my sister also was my best friend, playmate, partner-in-crime, and worst enemy.

Our family occupied the first floor of a two-story house in a small, gated community for nearly twenty years. At the center of this neighborhood, surrounded by two- and- four-story houses, was an empty lot of land that the children claimed as their playground. An old-fashioned well and an ancient, gigantic neem tree marked our neighborhood as one of a kind.

Neighbors were not just people who lived near me. They participated actively in my life. I was so close to the family next door—our kitchens were separated by a common door—that I picked up their language, Bengali, and conversed with them in their mother tongue. They nicknamed me "Bonny" and Joy "Puthush." The family that lived below us loved, fed, and patiently tolerated Joy and me as we transformed from energetic toddlers to unpredictable teenagers. Our neighbors stood by us through sicknesses and sorrow and celebrated our birthdays and baptisms. They were surrogates for extended family.

As for my literal extended family, my parents' lives crisscrossed with their siblings', creating a web of relationships that cocooned my childhood years. My sister and I spent our weekends and holidays hanging out with cousins at an aunt or uncle's house.

If it truly takes a village to raise a child, then my church was at the center of my village. From the ages of three to twenty-five, I called a local Methodist church home. Members of this small church lived within a radius of one to two miles. Familiarity, acceptance, and Christ-like love made this church a safe place for me. In a country where Christians were the minority, having Christian friends who shared common interests and passions fostered solidarity and community.

I was deeply rooted in the same soil, same geographical area for almost three decades of my life. Hyderabad was my world, my fishbowl. Family, neighbors, classmates, college friends, work colleagues, and ministry coworkers congregated in this tight space, leaving their fingerprints all over me and shaping my identity and worldview. I swam without worry in the security and comfort of my fishbowl. Neither predators nor tsunamis threatened the status quo.

In summer 2008, after a dreamlike whirlwind of a romance that lasted less than a year, I married Simon, and within three months, followed him to America. (Immigrants and foreigners commonly refer to the US as America.)

And everything changed.

Uprooted from Home

I became a trailing spouse, a term defined by the Cambridge Dictionary as "the husband or wife of an employee who is sent to work in another country." Simon's company assigned to him a project with a client based in Southern California. We arrived in Redondo Beach, a suburb of Los Angeles, in October 2008.

At first, I approached the opportunity with enthusiasm. As a lovestruck newlywed, I looked forward to the adventure of starting life together with my husband in a foreign country. I was keen to see the world-famous sights of America: Disneyland, Statue of Liberty, Niagara Falls, and the Grand Canyon, among many. I hoped to explore new places and make new friends. I embarked upon my journey to the West with an open mind, brimming with optimism and excitement.

Little did I know that the thrill would be short-lived. As months passed, I started to feel the real impacts of migration. The pain, brought on by the magnitude of change, became inescapable. Almost everything in my life had been replaced or removed. Surroundings were different and unfamiliar. I did not have any friends. Nor did I have a church community. Family was thousands of miles away. I wasn't prepared to handle the deluge of changes.

The stress of being uprooted became palpable when winter brought more winds of change. Christmas was in the air. Dark clouds of homesickness settled on the one-bedroom beachfront apartment that Simon and I called home in Southern California.

December in India was such a busy time that our calendars exploded with activities and appointments. Like most Christians in Hyderabad, we ushered in the Christmas season by putting up a giant, star-shaped paper lantern in front of our house and decorating our Christmas tree.

In the weeks leading up to Christmas, the kitchen buzzed with the busyness of a restaurant kitchen. My mother spent days whipping up large quantities of traditional Christian goodies such as *rose cookies* (rose-shaped fried donuts) and *murukulu* (fried lentil snack) and baking Christmas cakes. On Christmas day, our neighbors each received a small round cake, one per family, and so did other friends of the family.

Local churches brought their own unique flavor to Christmas by hosting family nights, community events, musical programs, or theatrical productions. The young people of our church participated enthusiastically in mission-based programs throughout the city. The preholiday celebrations culminated in a grand church service that took place either on Christmas Eve or Christmas morning.

Our non-Christian neighbors joined in our festivities without complaining about the commotion caused by loud carolers who showed up at our doorstep at odd hours of the night during the holiday season. They did not consider it impolite to drop into our home uninvited on Christmas day to hang out with us. Christmas was, by far, a community affair rather than a family affair.

My first Christmas in America was devoid of the people, traditions, and customs intrinsically tied to Christmas for as long as I could remember. Our Californian apartment was eerily quiet and deserted. No large tins of *rose cookies*. No guests at home. Though the streets outside were lit up with hundreds of lights and lamps and Christmas trees, Santa and reindeer inflatables, and nativity scenes appeared at every turn and corner, all I could see and feel was emptiness and gloom.

In December 2008, I came face-to-face with the reality that I had left behind more than a country. I felt the sharp pangs of being separated from the socket of home and familiarity. The pain cut to the core of my inner being. The inevitable crisis of identity stared right at me and I had to deal with it.

Identity Crisis

Identity is fragile, easily shaken or wrecked by relationships and experiences. The realization of who we are gives our life meaning and purpose. Our identity helps us find community. It feeds our self-worth and promotes our self-esteem. It helps us navigate the difficult terrain of life and determines how we respond to adversity and injustice. Knowing who we are and being secure in our identity also impacts our ability to raise a strong and healthy family. A strong and secure identity lays the foundation for a productive and joyful life.

For most of us, the search for identity is implicit and lifelong, something we don't even realize we are doing, even as every little action adds to our journey of self-discovery. Identity quest also can be deliberate, specific, and urgent.

Either way, the journey we take to find ourselves, though difficult, is inescapable and important and most often prompted by changes in the status quo.

Migration or displacement is only one of several reasons that can trigger an identity crisis. Sometimes, we don't have to physically move at all to feel displaced and disoriented. Feelings of not belonging or being accepted can thrive even in the minds of those who are firmly rooted in one place. Maybe the people we have loved have walked out on us. Maybe a sudden illness or injury has limited our ability to work and serve. Maybe someone we trust to protect us has harmed or abused us. These experiences can make us question ourselves. We may wonder if we are worthy of being loved and accepted, if our lives are meaningful, or if we even matter to anyone.

Migration Is a Stressor

My identity crisis surprised me, as I had not anticipated that migration would take a toll on me. I remember longing to travel and see the world as a young girl. I wanted to explore the world and experience new cultures. I believed, naively, that settling in America as a thirty-year-old adult would not be difficult. Imagine my surprise when I found myself struggling to adapt to life in a foreign land.

My upbringing in India was less traditional. I did not dress in *salwar-kameez* all the time and enjoyed eating a variety of cuisines, not just Indian. Reading American literature and watching American TV shows made me aware of Western culture. I grew up in urban India, where English was widely spoken. Immersing oneself in a culture, however, is not the same as knowing a culture and studying about it through books and TV. Assimilation requires courage and openness, a certain level of comfort with change and adventure, and a willingness to make mistakes and learn from them.

I was too afraid to fumble and stumble. I knew the language, but I was unfamiliar with the nuances in social mores and etiquette. Simple transactions at grocery shops and malls involved polite exchange of pleasantries: "How are you?" "Thank you," and "You're welcome." Indians are quite matter-of-fact with their daily dealings, eliminating the need for small talk or even polite smiles. What Indians consider impolite—for instance, calling someone older by their first name—is culturally appropriate in America. Eating with fingers is unthinkable and unhygienic by American standards. In many countries, including India, eating with hands is the norm.

As a new immigrant, I became more and more aware of my "otherness." Socially, I felt awkward and uncomfortable as I navigated through everyday activities.

Back home, I blended in. Here, I stood out.

Back home, I was in the majority. Here, I was the minority—by far.

Back home, I belonged. Here, I just didn't fit in.

Migration stripped away everything that defined me, making me feel worthless and insignificant.

I emigrated to America determined to support my husband's career, but I grieved the loss of my own. When we first came to America, Simon worked on a time-bound project in Southern California that could last anywhere between six months to a year. I hesitated to settle for a temporary job. Since I had come to the US on a dependent visa—as the spouse of someone who was authorized to work—I had to apply for a work permit, and the process could have taken months. Not having a driver's license severely restricted my choices even more. I used to pride myself on being an independent and self-made woman in India, but I grappled with being dependent on my spouse and not being employed in my new country.

My self-worth and self-esteem nosedived.

Before leaving India, I had been hired by a chain of fitness studios to handle their business development. I was involved in a vibrant youth ministry at my home church, mentoring young people. My friendships, in the workplace, church, neighborhood, and community, that were cultivated over time and trials, were my safety net, as well as great sources of joy and fulfillment.

I found myself in a foreign country where, all of a sudden, nobody knew me. Worse, nobody knew *about* me. My history, both good and bad, did not matter. Anonymity wiped my slate clean, socially and professionally.

Over the next few years, I followed my husband from one American city to another because of work assignments that lasted between six to eighteen months in each city. I attempted to fill the void in me with fun and frolic, but I couldn't shake off an underlying melancholy and emptiness. I fought every day to mimic the joy and cheer that I had previously so freely exuded. Not knowing what to do with myself and how to adapt to such a big change shook the foundations of my identity.

The process of adapting to another culture, or acculturation, compounded my crisis further. I felt like a mediator, constantly negotiating terms of contract between two warring voices in my head—the Indian voice, trying to hold on to my Indian values, and the immigrant voice, cheering me on to embrace American culture. Letting go of deep-rooted aspects of my ethnic and national identity made me wonder who I was becoming.

I turned into someone I didn't recognize. Was that a good thing, or not? I certainly had no way of telling.

Coping with Crisis

A few months into my life as a new immigrant in California, finally fed up with pitying myself, I resolved to make the most of my situation. *Life can't be so bad! I live in Los Angeles, the land of entertainment. I can certainly find things to see and do.* I tried to make the best use of my time when my husband went to work.

I went on long walks along Redondo Beach as often as I could, allowing the ocean to temporarily wash away my troubles. I watched hours of American TV (*Jerry Springer! Cheaters!*) with shock and fascination. During the weekends, my husband and I spent time discovering the new city we had come to call home. We sampled new restaurants in the area and took mini-vacations out of town.

A dance studio located within a short distance of our residence offered a variety of dance lessons. I did not let the abysmal public transport of Los Angeles keep me from staying connected to the one thing that gave me great pleasure and in a profound way linked me to my previous role in my home church as a choreographer—dancing. I took dance lessons three times a week, eager to learn as much as I could and also determined to use my time productively.

I also signed up to help with shelter dogs. I wrote emergency preparedness documents for a local nonprofit so I could feel useful and validated. I volunteered to write articles on fitness for an upcoming youth fitness center. Researching and writing on health topics took my mind away from my identity crisis, which was deepening and widening at a fast rate beneath the surface.

No matter what I did, however, my problems did not disappear. The more I immersed myself in work or entertainment, the more I realized that they were never going to hold the answer to my problems. Deep down, I was aware of a God-shaped hole in my life. All I had to do was run into God's arms, barefoot and messy, like the prodigal son who returned home to his loving father.

But I didn't return home to my Father.

I roamed aimlessly, thinking I could figure things out on my own. I ignored the still voice that kept reminding me that only an intimate relationship with God could fill the void in my soul and offer the right perspective on the changes happening around and within me.

Trusting God with Change

Changes, both big and small, sudden and planned, have the extraordinary capacity to disorient us. Even the strongest of Christians can wrestle with the storms brought on by unforeseen or difficult circumstances. The sudden death of a spouse, the loss of a child, the breakup of close relationships, a rough period of financial insecurity, the loss of a job, a divorce, and other life-altering events disrupt the status quo. Changes can test the sturdiness of our identity and shake the pillars of faith that define our relationship with God.

Many of us, therefore, resist change with all our strength and faculties. Transitions can turn our lives upside down, making us feel less loved and more alienated, less significant and more worthless, less appreciated and more useless. We dislike being pushed into a period of unwanted and unwelcome change as it compels us to reinvent ourselves.

It is during these transitions, however, that we need God the most. To reaffirm our identity in Him. To keep our eyes fixed on our purpose. To find strength and encouragement to press on. But instead of holding on to Him, some of us find ourselves fighting our dependence on Him and wanting to take charge of the situation. Our instinct is to fix the problem ourselves. Our natural response is to cry foul, hunker down, or stubbornly refuse to accept the change.

The Israelites, too, were inept at change management, even if the change was for their own good. Transitioning out of four hundred years of oppression into freedom should have made them grateful and solid believers. It did, but only for a short while.

Sojourning in the desert tested the mettle of God's people. Hunger and thirst, inhospitable terrain, unfamiliar surroundings, and a disintegration of their former lifestyle and habits stretched their faith in God. The Israelites threw tantrums, stamping their feet and shaking their fists at Moses and God. They incited God's anger by grumbling against Him.

Reminiscing on their days in Egypt as slaves, they had the audacity to think that their lives were better in Egypt than as free people delivered by the hand of God: "The Israelites said to them, 'If only we had died by the LORD's hand in Egypt! There we sat around pots of meat and ate all the food we wanted, but you have brought us out into this desert to starve this entire assembly to death'" (Exodus 16:3).

The freed people quickly forgot how they cried out to God in desperation, pleading with Him to deliver them from the Pharaoh's brutal regime. God had unleashed His power against Egypt and rescued His people by sending plagues and parting the Red Sea. Their deliverance sealed their identity as God's chosen people.

The Israelites were aware of who they were—a nation set apart for God, with a blessed spiritual ancestry and heritage. But an unknown future and nomadic living pushed them out of their comfort zone, making them anxious and insecure. Everything around them was different. They, too, were being transformed into a free nation, ready to occupy the promised land. However, the Israelites could not accept the change with gratitude and enthusiasm. They lacked faith in God's promises.

God Is the Only Constant in Change

God's people failed to see that though the land underneath their feet had shifted, the God in heaven, the God of their forefathers, the God of Abraham, Jacob, and Isaac, hadn't changed. God's nature and promises are immutable.

> God is not human, that he should lie,
> > not a human being, that he should change his mind.
> Does he speak and then not act?
> > Does he promise and not fulfill?
> > > (Numbers 23:19)

All they had to do was focus their eyes on Him. His promise to make them into a great nation still stood true. And He would provide for them in the wilderness, gently leading and guiding them to Canaan, the promised land.

Like the Israelites, migration was the stressor that tested my faith and unleashed a crisis of identity. I took my eyes off God's unrelenting love and never-changing faithfulness, and obsessed over my ever-changing circumstances. By not looking upward and by looking too closely inward, I wandered deeper into the wilderness where the search for identity turned into a lonely and futile journey.

Staying focused on God's unchangeable nature is the only thing that can help us weather the storms of change and keep our identity intact in Christ. When we dwell on His steadfast love, His comfort and strength become real and present. His promises give hope. Fixing our thoughts on God, the only constant in a transient life, keeps us from being swept away by winds of change. A crisis of identity can become an opportunity, or a gift that sparks spiritual growth and creativity.

Reach In

1. How do you react to changes or transitions in your life?

_____

2. What particular aspect of change do you struggle with or find challenging?

_____

3. What change or event in your life is forcing you to alter your way of life or reinvent yourself?

---

4. When you look back at your life, can you identify situations or events that have impacted your identity?

---

5. Which verses from the Bible can you meditate upon to help you remember that God is the only constant in change?

Reach Out

Is there anyone in your family or circle of friends who is going through a difficult transition? Take some time out of your schedule to connect with your friend or family member and ask how she or he is doing. Remind her or him of God's unchanging faithfulness and promises.

Reach Up

Dear Father in Heaven,

I'm in awe of Your unchanging nature. You are the God of Abraham, Isaac, and Jacob. You are the God who brought the Israelites out of Egypt through the miraculous parting of the Red Sea. You performed wonders to rescue Your people. You led them to the promised land and You kept Your covenant with them. You remained faithful to Your chosen people. I'm amazed and humbled that You are my God. Thank You for all the promises You gave me through Your Word. When changes rock my world, help me to stand on Your promises and not be shaken. May Your Word protect me and keep me secure. Help me to meditate on your steadfast love and great faithfulness in good as well as bad times. May I place my trust in Your character and not in people or places. As I encounter difficult changes and go through transitions, change me from the inside out so I become more like You.

Amen.

CHAPTER 2
The Skein of Identity

The LORD is my rock, my fortress and my deliverer;
my God is my rock, in whom I take refuge,
my shield and the horn of my salvation, my stronghold.

Psalm 18:2

While shopping alone for summer clothes for my five-year-old son at Target, I craved a cold drink. I greeted the employee at the Starbucks counter. "I'll have the Strawberry Acai Refresher, please."

The employee frowned. "Excuse me?"

"May I have a Strawberry Acai Refresher, please."

She sighed. "Excuse me?"

I repeated my order slowly. "Strawberry Acai Refresher. Tall."

"I can't understand you, ma'am." She shook her head.

I felt the gazes of people around me pivot in our direction. Was I imagining things, or did the coffee shop grow suddenly quiet? Could everyone hear our exchange?

I tried one more time. "I would like to order the Strawberry Acai Refresher, please."

"You have to be clearer. I don't understand you." She came closer to me, tilted her head to one side, and cupped her ear, as if she wanted me to pour my words into her ear.

I fought back the tears. I pointed to the drink on the menu hanging on the wall and tried again.

"Straw-be-rry Acai Re-fresh-err, please. Do you understand?"

She quoted the price without making eye contact.

I paid for my drink and noticed the line behind me had grown longer.

The employee looked at the man standing behind me and said, "Next!"

No smile. No apology.

I moved to the side and quickly grabbed my drink when it was ready, averting eye contact from the long line of people. I raced to my car as fast as I could. I stuffed the Cat and Jack shorts and T-shirts in the trunk. I turned on the ignition to start the car and tears rushed down my cheeks. Flashbacks of the incident kept coming back to me, drowning out the car radio. The words. The looks of people. The tone of the employee. I did not stop crying till I reached home.

I wanted to tell the Starbucks employee that English was my primary language, and I was good at it. I wanted to let her know that I was fluent not only in English but also two Indian languages. I wanted her to know that I had won elocution and essay writing contests in school, both in English and Hindi. None of that seemed to matter.

Communicating my feelings and thoughts was never a problem for me. In India, if someone did not understand English, I spoke in Hindi. If I was still unable to get through, I tried Telugu. I switched languages depending on the need of the hour, like many other Indians.

The first time someone told me my English was good, I was baffled. I was raised in a multilingual home. English was the language of instruction in my school. I went to an English church, worshipped in English, and read my Bible in English. The language of business at my workplaces in India was English. I neither learned English in America nor do I speak English with an American accent. But I'm able to express myself better in English than in any other language. It did not occur to me, till I came to live in America, that my diction and accent set me apart as an ethnic minority.

For the most part, however, I was able to converse fairly well with my American friends. By and large, I found Americans to be understanding and accepting of my unrolled *r*'s and overemphasized *t*'s. But the incident at Starbucks highlighted the fact that certain markers of my identity, such as my outward appearance and the way I spoke, not only made me stand out in my new homeland, but also made me feel more self-conscious and less self-confident.

The Skein of Identity

I think of identity markers as fibers or threads that are intricately woven together to form the skein of identity. Upbringing, family, physical appearance, cuisine, music, language, community, faith, ministry, and profession are some of the important threads that comprise the skein of our identity.

Identity is fluid and changes with age and circumstances. Old threads can be replaced with new ones. As routines and patterns of the familiar get established, more threads are added to the skein of identity, or existing threads are reinforced. Becoming a parent, for instance, adds a strong thread to the skein. Parenthood influences how we see ourselves and determines the choices we make in the interest of our children and families. When our children grow up and start raising their own families, or when we retire, we can be driven to reinvent ourselves.

Some of the threads of the skein become so integral and central to our identity that when they get unraveled, frayed, or replaced, we come face-to-face with a crisis where the entire skein begins to come apart. If, for instance, the thread of profession became the heart of our identity, any change to our professional situation would completely disorient us. We could even find our personal life, friendships, and habits thrown into a tizzy until we have regained our professional balance.

The skein of identity can also be tightly wound around the thread of family. We can define ourselves solely based on our roles as parents or spouses. Some of us draw our significance and self-worth from our material possessions. For others, status in society and financial standing become the strongest threads in the skeins of their identity.

If a difficult situation or a sudden change takes away several of the threads at once from the skein, we can find ourselves decimated, brought back to square one, forced to face the most basic question—*Who am I?*

That was my crisis. I was fortunate to have made the move to America voluntarily with my spouse. I didn't have to contend with trauma of forced displacement faced by refugees. Still, the stress of displacement and resettlement hit me hard. It tugged at almost every thread that came together to form the skein of my identity: looks and language, culture and community, and family and faith. The threads in my skein did not just unravel, they were systematically being disintegrated, picked at, and torn apart.

I remember the first time I walked into an Indian grocery store in California after we left India. The smell of cumin, coriander, red chilies, turmeric, and *garam masala* filled the air. My mouth did not stop watering. The shelves were lined with products that were familiar to me. I almost cried when I spotted *Maggi noodles*, a ramen kind of snack that was my comfort food at home. I smiled ear to ear while I walked around the store. Like a child at a candy store, I filled my cart excitedly, grabbing every food item that reminded me of home, of who I used to be. My eyes watered too.

Indian food both soothed and fueled my homesickness. Even after a decade of living in America, Indian restaurants have a dramatic effect on my senses. They lift my spirits because my ethnic cuisine is an important aspect of who I am—my upbringing and culture. The sights, smells, and flavors of Indian food resurrect memories that involve life-changing events and people most precious to me.

When I moved to America, both tangible and intangible markers or threads of my identity were almost all lost, impelling me to replace them with new ones. In short, I had to put together my identity skein from scratch. Alone in a new country, Simon and I had to find proxy families. We invested time and energy in forging new friendships. We church-hopped to find a new community of believers. We acquired new cultural mannerisms and tastes. Reconstructing our identities was challenging and painful, but necessary.

Job's Skein Comes Apart

The book of Job tells the story of Job's remarkable faith during a time of great adversity, when almost all the threads of his identity came apart without warning.

Job was such a righteous and upright man that God challenged Satan to test his faith by afflicting him with undeserved pain and suffering (Job 1:8–12). Consider the magnitude of Job's loss and sorrow when he was attacked by Satan—not one of his seven sons, three daughters, 7,000 sheep, 3,000 camels, 500 oxen, 500 donkeys, and countless number of servants survived the sudden enemy raids and natural disasters (Job 1:2–3, 13–19). Afflicted with painful sores all over his body, Job also suffered physically (Job 2:7).

In a single day, Job went from being a beloved father, a respected member of the community, and a wealthy and successful businessman to becoming a childless man, stripped of his good standing and possessions. Everything that made him feel loved, accepted, valued, and important was annihilated—overnight.

No doubt, Job wrestled with the sudden calamity and unfair suffering. But instead of cursing God and walking away from Him, Job chose to lean into Him and trust Him. He directed his lament toward God in reverent worship.

Even when all the threads of Job's skein were violently ripped away, he remained "blameless and upright" (Job 1:8). He praised God in the midst of the worst time of his life. Through the tears and sores, Job acknowledged that all his material blessings came from a sovereign God, both in times of plenty as well as in times of lack.

Satan wrongly assumed that Job was devoted to God only because of the blessings God bestowed on him—health, wealth, and family. Satan wrongly believed that Job's sense of security lay in his material possessions and that his identity was wrapped around people and things. The enemy took away everything from Job, including his own health, but he could not lay a finger on Job's righteousness, his relationship with God. The thread of faith in Job's skein remained strong and thick.

For those who don't know the story of Job, it ends well. God not only restored but also multiplied Job's wealth (Job 42:10, 12). He had ten more children and lived a long and prosperous life. He was able to put the pieces of his life back together, emerging from the wilderness with a denser thread of faith. Almost every thread of his skein was replaced with a new thread, one stronger and better than the former one. Job was able to reconstruct his identity by drawing strength from his faith. His renewed identity and new life were based on and derived from his personal relationship with God.

Like Job, a strong thread of faith can help us endure and overcome suffering with the skein of our identity undamaged. We can cling to Jesus and lean on Him to fortify our faith because He is the "author and finisher of our faith" (Hebrews 12:2 KJV). He is the source of our faith (2 Peter 1:1). We receive faith not because we earn it but because of His grace.

When Jesus's disciples asked Him to increase their faith, Jesus replied, "If you have faith as a mustard seed, you can say to this mulberry tree, 'Be pulled up by the roots and be planted in the sea,' and it would obey you" (Luke 17:6 NKJV). His answer implies that the quantity of faith is immaterial. Who or what we put our faith in matters most. Jesus is not only the source but also the object of our faith. Putting our faith in Him means we rely on Him rather than our own abilities or other people for help during tough circumstances. When Jesus becomes the center of our attention and affection, the foundation of our identity holds and does not collapse under pressure.

God not only put us together, cell by cell, in our mothers' wombs (Psalm 139:13) but also preordained the threads of our identities. He determined where we would be born, how we would be raised, and what language we would speak. Except for the thread of our faith, almost all other threads in our skein are temporary, damageable, and replaceable. But our faith in God is long-lasting since He is immutable.

The story of Joseph's life illustrates how the thread of faith can keep the skein of our identity intact even when we lose almost all of our threads.

Joseph's Thread of Faith

Joseph, the youngest of twelve brothers, was around seventeen years old when he was sold into slavery by his brothers who were enraged by their father's favoritism and Joseph's preposterous dreams. Joseph arrived in Egypt as a slave, stripped of all his belongings and relationships. The only thing that he brought with him to a foreign land was his faith in God.

Forced to start his life from scratch, Joseph became an outstanding slave to Potiphar, an Egyptian official who put him in charge of his household. The Egyptian saw the Lord was with Joseph and credited his success to Joseph's God (Genesis 39:3–6). All the markers of Joseph's identity were destroyed, but the thread of faith not only remained unscathed but seemed to be getting stronger. Suffering did not take Joseph away from the Lord. Rather, it drove him toward Him.

Wrongly accused of preying upon Potiphar's wife, Joseph's hopes of rebuilding a life for himself in Egypt were crushed when he was imprisoned. But even in prison, people took notice of Joseph as a man of God. The warden of the prison put him in charge of everything because he witnessed God's favor upon the young man. Through a series of remarkable events, the Pharoah of Egypt elevated Joseph to a position of leadership since he believed Joseph had the Spirit of God in him (Genesis 41:38).

At the age of thirty, thirteen years after he left his country and his people, the former Israelite slave became the second most powerful man in Egypt. Though he put down roots in a foreign country, gained a new family, and established a new career, Joseph's spiritual identity did not change or break down. He was subjected to unfairness and injustice, again and again, by loved ones and strangers, but he trusted the God of his father and forefathers and depended on His covenantal love.

God preserved Joseph's life and made his broken life whole again. Joseph was able to reunite with Jacob and his brothers. Through Joseph's adversity and success, God helped the Egyptians, Jacob's family, and the people of several nations survive a terrible period of drought and famine. God used Joseph to save lives and preserve the seed of Abraham.

Joseph's secure faith was central to his identity. For most of his adult life, though he was an Egyptian ruler, he served God until his final breath. He knew that God had promised his ancestors that He would bless their descendants and give them Canaan as their inheritance. Joseph's belief in God's promises solidified the core of his identity.

Joseph's story made me ponder on the veracity of my faith and how it had evolved over the years. I had no doubt that my faith was indestructible and unsinkable, until I came face-to-face with the ugly consequences of immigration. After all, I had known God to be my Lord since I was a little child. I'd endured the ups and downs of life with Him by my side. Certainly, there was no way my boat could sink, no matter what storm came my way.

My Spiritual Origins

I was brought up in a loving, Christian home. My mother was the spiritual matriarch of the house. She led us in family devotions every night. Pastors and ministers visited our home frequently, an important part of pastors' duties in India at that time. My sister and I were expected to drop whatever toys we were playing with or peel ourselves away from our favorite television shows to pay full attention to the pastors when they expounded the Scriptures and prayed for our family.

During one of those pastoral visits, I got down on my knees and accepted Jesus into my heart, fascinated by the picture of heaven that the pastor had painted and terrified by the images of fiery furnaces in hell. I do not remember my exact age, but I was certainly not older than ten.

My mother was in charge of youth ministry, and then later, VBS ministry at a local church. As a child, I spent several hours hanging out with church leaders and volunteers, traveling pastors, and parachurch leaders. I was not allowed to skip Sunday school, even if my tummy hurt. Occasionally, we traveled to the far end of the city to attend the weekly fellowship at YWAM (Youth with a Mission).

As I grew older, my faith in God grew, despite the teenage mood swings and acne. It was not until I suffered a terrible heartbreak in my early twenties that I realized how great my need was for an intimate relationship with God. This became one of the major turning points of my life.

I flourished in God's garden of love and grace when He restored my broken heart. As a single woman, I fell in love with God in a fresh, new way, making it my life's goal to serve Him faithfully with my time and talents. My priority was to grow in the Lord, to get to know Him better. I spent long hours in my bedroom worshipping God and journaling my meditations. I consumed Christian literature with urgency and filled my ears with worship music. Mentoring young people at my church became a passion. I took delight in sharing God's Word and my story with anyone who would listen.

A few years later, God brought my husband into my life. Simon and I both came from different cultural backgrounds but had much in common when it came to our spiritual upbringing and values. Convinced we were made for each other, we tied the knot within a year of dating. Shortly after the wedding and the honeymoon, we moved to America.

Securing the Thread of Faith

Relocating to a foreign country and living as an immigrant exposed the true condition of my faith. I discovered with disappointed amazement that my identity in Christ had a weak foundation. I thought that God was at the center of my life, that He was the most important thing to me, and that everything else came second compared to Him. But my faith was not as solid as I professed it to be. And I was afraid to admit that truth to myself.

I could easily profess that Christ was the love of my life as long as I was living in the comfort of my own home and country and when everything around seemed comfortable, familiar, and permanent. I considered my life surrendered wholly to God as long as I felt safe, secure, and intact within my own community and culture. I could trust Him in everything as long as my needs were being met through loved ones and precious things. Growing in the Lord was the only reasonable outcome as long as my faith was attached to my role and service in my home church.

When every part of me was stripped away and taken apart, and I was lying bare and exposed, I could not bring myself to say, "Christ is more than enough for me."

Only after a few years did I fully appreciate how God was using my identity crisis to refine and strengthen my faith. I was too preoccupied with my problems to have the right perspective. My self-centeredness made me oblivious to His plans and purposes. In vain, I searched for strength within myself to overcome my problems. Instead of turning my attention toward God and seeking direction from Him, I looked outside, to the world, for answers and for help.

My immigrant experience revealed that the thread of faith is integral to the skein of identity. The stronger the thread, the more secure my identity is. I learned from the parable of the wise and foolish builders (Matthew 7:24–29) that a life centered around Jesus can successfully withstand losses, injustice, sickness, persecution, and brokenness. This centeredness can only be achieved by spending time with Him, listening and talking to Him.

Jesus urges us to lay the foundation of our lives upon Him. He says, "As for everyone who comes to me and hears my words and puts them into practice, I will show you what they are like. They are like a man building a house, who dug down deep and laid the foundation on rock" (Luke 6:47–48).

When we cling to the thread of faith in the face of adversity, God deepens our faith, grows our affection for Him, and causes hope to thrive in our hearts. Important threads in our skein may be frayed or lost. But we can trust that God will replace our threads with new ones—better and stronger. And we will be transformed. We will become more like Him.

Reach In

1. Which aspects of your life do you consider to be most integral to your identity?

2. How would you respond if one or more threads in the skein of your identity were to come apart?

_____

3. What difficult situation or relationship is currently testing your faith and making you question your identity?

_____

4. Why is spending time with God important to you? What blessings have you experienced by spending time in prayer and Bible study?

_____

5. What steps can you take to secure your trust in God and His promises?

_____

Reach Out

Write a note of encouragement to a friend who has recently suffered a loss. Include a list of promises from the Bible to encourage her or him.

Reach Up

Dear Father in Heaven,

My faith in You is my treasure, my sustenance, my strength. You are my all in all. You give me identity. May I cling to You when changes upend my life. May I trust in You and Your promises when life seems unfair and cruel. Help me to look to Your steadfast love and anchor my heart in Your faithfulness. I thank You for helping me endure many trials. Thank You for using them to refine my faith. Continue to preserve and grow my faith. Make my faith in You so noticeable and remarkable that people around me will be inspired to get to know You and put their trust in You.

Amen.

CHAPTER 3
God Shapes Identity

*For he chose us in him before the creation of the world to
be holy and blameless in his sight. In love he predestined
us for adoption to sonship through Jesus Christ, in
accordance with his pleasure and will.*

Ephesians 1:4–5

Bend and stretch. Bend and stretch.

I bent my arms at the elbows and stretched them out, hoping
to relieve the strain I felt as I lugged my large suitcase along the
hilly terrain of the resort. The early morning flight to Colorado and
the long drive from the airport to the resort left me tired. My feet
wobbled and shifted. The altitude was high; my fitness level was
abysmal. Panting and puffing, I dragged myself uphill. I regretted
all those times I stayed at home instead of going to Zumba class.

With every step that took me closer to my room at the top
of the hill, my heartbeat pounded louder and louder, not only
with exhaustion but also with excitement. My mind buzzed with
thoughts about the workshops I would attend and the people I
hoped to meet at my first writers' conference.

I stopped to extract the last tissue from my pocket and wipe
the melting makeup from my face when I caught a glimpse of the
gorgeous Rocky Mountains. The beauty and magnificence of the
towering mountains snapped me out of my thoughts. The crisp,
fresh air washed over me, purifying my body and mind. I saw a
bunny scurry across a grass patch. An elk stared at me lazily from
a bush nearby. Mesmerized, I forgot about the conference and my
new adventures in writing. I allowed myself to be seduced by the
scenery. *I wish I could live here forever.*

And then, an employee at the resort interrupted my daydreaming.

"Excuse me, are you an international staffer?"

Shouldn't he be asking if I needed help? Instead, he stunned me with his line of interrogation, "Are you American?"

I've never been asked that question in my ten years of living in America, though I did mull over my nationality from time to time. I ignored his question. "I'm here as a guest for the writers' conference."

He smiled. "Sorry. I hope you have a good time at the conference."

When I finally reached the room, I had barely opened the door when I plopped onto the comfy bed. As I lay on my back and caught my breath, I pondered over my immigrant identity.

On most days, I forget what I look like. I go about my day as usual. It's only when I enter a restaurant or a room full of white people that I become aware of my brownness.

The employee meant no harm when he asked me if I was an international staffer. He was merely doing his job, politely and respectfully. My skin color, however, confused him. I learned that the resort often hired temporary foreign employees during the spring and summer every year. I rode with a few of them in the shuttle from the airport to the resort. While I saw myself as a conference attendee, this man saw me as someone who could be a foreign employee.

Looking Through the Lens of Others

How I looked began to matter to me more in America than it did in India. My skin color, though important to my identity, was something I never paid attention to before. But now, it became prominent, like the bulging tummy of a pregnant woman. Other tangible aspects of my identity, like language, mannerisms, food, and clothing, and intangible aspects like cultural and social values also came to the forefront.

Living as an immigrant heightened my awareness of how others regarded me. Not only that, I placed a high value on others' perception of me because it influenced how I saw myself. I had no way of confirming, though, what others thought of me. I assumed, for instance, that because I was not being productive, people considered me worthless or useless. They did not know my history—my education, work experience, or network of contacts. They must have thought I was unimportant, so I felt unimportant.

I also craved genuine friendships, having left behind all my close friends. I worked extra hard to win friends. I was from the East. I was different, I figured, from the Westerners. I was the newbie who never got old. Was it possible for anyone to look beyond stereotypes and connect with me? What could I do to make it easier for them to accept me, an outsider, as a friend?

Going back to India for short visits used to compound my confusion because I started to feel that I didn't belong even among my own people.

To some extent, immigrant or otherwise, some of us tend to see ourselves through the eyes of others who matter to us. Depending on our personality, we might have greater or lesser propensity to succumb to the image others have of us. When our frames of reference are externally derived, our identity is shaped by both how we see ourselves, intrinsically, and how others see us, extrinsically.

One of the biggest struggles of dealing with migration was that my life was colored by others' impressions of me. I was a misfit, eager to belong. I realized I had stopped seeing myself through God's eyes. Instead of going to God's Word for affirmation, I allowed my identity to be shaped by people's ratings and reviews of me. The source of my identity crisis was that I was looking to others for validation, acceptance, and security. My crisis turned into a burden I found increasingly hard to bear. Desperate and exhausted, I turned to the Bible for answers.

And I found Jesus.

Jesus's Secure Identity

Jesus was secure in His identity as the Son of God. In the Gospel of Luke, the genealogy of Jesus highlights His identity as fully human and fully divine by describing Jesus as "the son . . . of Joseph" (Luke 3:23) as well as "the son of Adam, the son of God" (Luke 3:38). Jesus's identity informed His ministry and mission.

The Bible does not give us too many details about Jesus's childhood. But the story about Jesus getting separated from His parents during the Passover gives us a glimpse of how Jesus viewed Himself even as an adolescent.

Jesus's family went to Jerusalem to celebrate the Passover, like they did every year. When the festival was over, Mary and Joseph embarked on their journey back home without noticing that Jesus had stayed back in the Holy City. After a day on the road, when they discovered Jesus was missing, they returned to search for their twelve-year-old boy.

Mary and Joseph were amazed to find Jesus questioning and listening to teachers of the Law in the temple. He seemed content and calm, while they were worked up about their missing child (Luke 2:46–48).

When they questioned Jesus, His answer perplexed them, "Why were you searching for me?" He asked. "Didn't you know that I had to be in my Father's house?" (Luke 2:49).

Jesus had a good grasp of His identity. His earthly father may have been Joseph, but He knew God was His heavenly Father. His identity dictated His overall purpose as well as his day-to-day living. He was at the temple because it was His Father's house. He simply had to be there on His Father's business.

But this truth was lost not only on his family (Luke 2:50) but also on his community. When Jesus started his ministry, His community identified him as just a carpenter, the son of Joseph (Luke 4:22). Some thought he was "a good man" (John 7:12). Others were not sure if He was a rabbi or the Messiah. Jesus's own brothers doubted Him (John 7:5). Most people did not know or understand Jesus's heavenly identity. It was difficult for them to comprehend that God's very own Son was walking among them, in flesh and blood. They could not imagine this marriage of the majestic and the mundane in the form of the Messiah they had been expecting to come.

Jesus did not let the confusion, unbelief, and skepticism of those around Him shake His identity. He didn't allow difficult circumstances to steer how He operated. He believed what God the Father said about Him in that audible public proclamation at His baptism, "And a voice came from heaven: 'You are my Son, whom I love; with you I am well pleased'" (Luke 3:22).

The voice of God booming like thunder in the sky was not meant to give Jesus confidence or peace of mind. It was for the benefit of the crowd, so they would know that Jesus was the Son of God. Again, during Jesus's transfiguration on Mount Hermon, God affirmed Jesus's identity, "A voice came from the cloud, saying, 'This is my Son, whom I have chosen; listen to him'" (Luke 9:35).

The same voice of God confirms and clarifies our identity. God speaks to us through His Word, declaring to us that we are His children, and that we, like Jesus, are chosen, loved, and given purpose by Him.

Salvation Gives Us New Identity

Our identity undergoes a dramatic reconstruction the moment we are saved. As believers who belong to the same family and kingdom of God, we share the same spiritual identity.

We were once sinners, prisoners of our carnal selves, and separated from God. Now, through Christ's sacrifice, we are set free from the power of sin, made righteous, and reconciled with God. When we lived as mortals under the curse of Adam, we were destined to pay for our sins with our lives. Now, we are put on a new path, one that offers abundant life on this earth and eternal life in the heaven to come.

There is a shift in the spiritual realm when we become God's children, His special possession. He regenerates and transforms us when we submit ourselves to His authority. We become a new creation. We gain a new identity (2 Corinthians 5:17).

Our new identity is anchored to Christ, not to our family, profession, country, or culture. It cannot be altered, negotiated, or withdrawn. Our spiritual identity is permanent and secure.

We are *children* of God (John 1:12).
We are *heirs* of God (Romans 8:17).
We are *loved* by God (1 John 3:1).
We are *chosen* by God (Ephesians 1:4).
We are *redeemed* by God (Ephesians 1:7).
We are *a holy people* (Deuteronomy 7:6).
We are a *royal priesthood* (1 Peter 2:9).

These biblical truths are the building blocks of a believer's spiritual DNA. As God's treasure, we can do nothing to become less valuable or precious in His sight. We do not have to base our identity on our own performance and good works or on others' opinions of us. Securing our identity in Christ frees us from the trap of pleasing people and earning approval and praise from them.

Not only that, but our identity also energizes us to participate in God's plans. It keeps us moving forward in our faith journey. The knowledge that God lavishes spiritual blessings on us (Ephesians 1:3) gives us strength and hope to face trials and temptations. Our identity emboldens us to take giant leaps of faith because we do not operate in our own strength or wisdom but depend on the Holy Spirit to supply us with everything we need to accomplish His plans.

The Power of a Secure Identity

A closer examination of "a man after [God's] own heart" (Acts 13:22), the greatest king of Israel, David, can shed light on the power of embracing our identity, inspiring us to face the giants in our life with confidence and courage.

When David's father sends him to the battlefield to check on his brothers, David is only a young man. At the battlefield, he notices a standoff between the armies of Israel and Philistine. The Philistine giant, Goliath, taunts the Israelites and their God. He challenges them to a duel to decide the outcome of the war. Because the Israelites believe that none of them stand a chance against the giant, they become terrified, lose all hope, and fear defeat.

But David, a shepherd with no military training or background, volunteers to fight Goliath. He convinces the king of

Israel, Saul, that it was God who helped him fight and kill wild animals in defense of his sheep and that God would enable him also to kill Goliath.

The shepherd boy is unafraid to take on a mighty warrior since he associates himself with the armies of the living God. "Who is this uncircumcised Philistine that he should defy the armies of the living God?" (1 Samuel 17:26). Even though he did not serve in the Israelite army, he sees himself as a warrior of God's army, equipped with the weapon of faith to defend God's people. David knows he serves a mighty God who protects and rescues His people. He does not consider his age, physical ability, profession, training, or experience as impediments when he decides to take up Goliath's challenge.

God delivers Goliath into David's hands not through the use of sophisticated weapons but through a shepherd's sling and a few stones.

David believed that God could use him to save the Israelite army from destruction. He believed in his identity as an Israelite, a citizen of a nation that bore God's name. The battle was neither his nor Israel's to fight. The battle belonged to the Lord (1 Samuel 17:47), who was the real king of Israel.

Just like David, we can come face-to-face with a giant who can seem insurmountable. A debilitating physical injury, a divorce, the death of a loved one, being let go from a job, a sudden financial loss, or a hopeless diagnosis, among others. The troubles and trappings of this world can hinder God's words from reaching our ears and reminding us of who we are in Him. Crises can drown out God's voice.

But we can remind ourselves that the Holy Spirit who indwells us, empowers us, and encourages us to persevere and stand our ground. We can hold on to the truth that the battle belongs to the Lord and that He will rescue us from our predicament because we are His children and He loves us. We can resolve not to give into the narrative that we are weak and unworthy. Not good enough. Not strong enough. By faith, we can shut out these voices, believing in our God-given identity. God is capable of delivering us from whatever crisis comes our way. Standing on our identity in Christ we can overcome every battle we encounter.

Recognizing that our battle is spiritual is the first step toward securing our identity and victory.

Satan Is Out to Steal Our Identity

One of the enemy's strategies is to use difficult circumstances to cause confusion about our God-given identity. His goal is to make us doubt and question who we are in Christ. Satan used the same ploy when he tempted Jesus in the wilderness. By challenging Jesus's identity as the Son of God, the tempter tried to provoke Jesus to sin. But Jesus defended Himself against the enemy's attack by using Scripture tactfully to undo Satan.

To Satan's challenge, "If you are the Son of God, tell these stones to become bread" (Matthew 4:3b), Jesus replied, "It is written: 'Man shall not live on bread alone, but on every word that comes from the mouth of God'" (Matthew 4:4).

When Satan made Jesus stand on the highest point of the temple and tempted Him, "If you are the Son of God, throw yourself down" (Matthew 4:6a), Jesus answered, "It is also written: 'Do not put the Lord your God to the test'" (Matthew 4:7).

Jesus illustrates that being secure in our identity in God is crucial to overcoming temptation or adversity. When we are vulnerable and prone to wandering away from God, reminding ourselves of our spiritual identity will arm us with the strength and courage we need to stand firm and resist the enemy. We can defeat the enemy with the "sword of the Spirit," acknowledging that the battle belongs to the Lord (Ephesians 6:17). Because He is victorious, we are too. Not only can we face difficult circumstances with confidence, but we can also take bold steps of faith to serve God in mighty ways.

How God Sees Me

The challenges I faced as an immigrant drew me into a closer walk with God. I spent more and more time meditating on His Word, eager to get to know Him better. When I looked at myself through the lens of God's truth, He renewed and expanded my vision of the world around, but more importantly at this time, of myself.

I still wonder at the beauty of how this relationship works—an intimate relationship with God is the source from which I draw a picture of myself. Walking and talking with God reveals to me who He is, and that knowledge, in turn, shows me who I am. My quest for identity had taken a turn in the right direction.

It has been more than decade since I moved to America. I no longer consider myself a newbie. But I'm not fully immune to the enemy's attacks on my identity. Every now and then, I am easily swayed by people's approval or treatment of me. I let people's praise or criticism get to me and influence my feelings. But my immigrant experience has made me more mindful of such pitfalls. I've learned to read the signs and symptoms and take steps to strengthen my faith.

I draw myself closer to Jesus's side. I turn up the volume on a Christian podcast. I tune in to a Christian radio station. I bury myself in a Bible study. I call a friend and ask for prayer. Whatever it takes. I layer biblical truth upon truth upon my eyes and ears until I hear God's words in my heart and head, loud and clear. He loves me more than I can imagine. I am His. I belong to His family. I am a citizen of heaven, His kingdom. I am His daughter and friend.

Reach In

1. How have you let others affect the way you see yourself?

2. In what way can truths about your biblical identity transform your thought patterns and actions?

3. For what particular aspect of your God-given identity can you thank God for today?

4. What steps are you going to take to tune into God's voice so He can shape your identity?

---

5. What specific actions can you take today to remind yourself of what God says about you?

Reach Out

Tell someone today that God loves them. Affirm their God-given identity.

Reach Up

Dear Father in Heaven,

I thank You for loving me so much that You sent Your Son to die on the cross. Thank You for giving me a new life and a new identity. I am forgiven and made righteous through Jesus's sacrifice. I am loved and highly favored by You. I matter to You. You give my life purpose. My life is valuable since You breathed life into me and You saved me. When I feel unworthy and unloved, please help me remember that I'm Yours, loved and cherished by You. Hide me in You so that I am able to resist the enemy when he tells me I'm a nobody. May I always see myself through your eyes.

Amen.

CHAPTER 4
Citizenship in Heaven

But our citizenship is in heaven.
And we eagerly await a Savior from there,
the Lord Jesus Christ.

Philippians 3:20

Ryan and I were riding an elevator in a mall on one of our trips to India. Packed, as only Indians allow themselves to be packed, into that six-foot by six-foot square box with other shoppers, my five-year-old son felt absolutely and uncontrollably compelled to give voice to his thoughts. Right there. Right then. Out of the blue. Throwing me off guard.

"I am American, right, Mommy? Because I eat American food. I don't like Indian food."

Ryan searched my face for clarification or confirmation.

"We can talk about it later," I whispered. I felt my cheeks flush.

As my fellow elevator riders darted their glances at me, I did my best to avoid eye contact with them.

India was Ryan's luxury resort and spa. Every other year he got the chance to escape routine, school, and homework for a month-long vacation in the Indian subcontinent (a term that refers to South Asia) where his grandparents catered to his every whim. They considered his indiscretions cute. Aunts and uncles showered him with love, allowing him to indulge in mindless snacking and unrestrained TV watching. In India, Ryan blended in. At the same time, he was also aware of his foreignness, knowing that, culturally, he was different from his own flesh and blood.

A natural dilemma for most immigrant children is whether they should attach themselves to or consciously strip themselves of their parents' ethnic identity. My son will probably have more questions about his identity than I can answer or solve. Ironically, as someone who lives in between two cultures, I struggle with my own share of conflicting identities.

After living in the new homeland for almost a decade, I feel like I belong. I cannot, at the same time, resist the pull I feel toward my homeland. The umbilical cord has not yet been severed. My parents, sister, most of my relatives live in India, and I continue to be involved in their lives. I remain in touch with my Indian friends. It is unthinkable to cut off contact from India altogether. At the same time, I gather new friends in America, and some of them have become so close that I consider them family.

For the most part, it seems as if I am stuck between two worlds, sandwiched by two cultures, sometimes believing that I belong to neither. Acceptance and exclusion seem to remarkably coexist, making it harder for me to settle the issue of my national identity.

The ambiguity in my status as an immigrant accentuates an important aspect of my identity that I have previously overlooked and ignored—my identity as a spiritual immigrant. Physically, we are earthlings, with both cradle and coffin grounded in earth. But, spiritually, our new birth and identity in Christ changes our status from a native of this world to a foreigner. We are not only the beloved and chosen children of God and coheirs with Christ, but also members of the kingdom of God with the full rights and privileges of citizenship.

We do not belong to this world ("I have given them your word and the world has hated them, for they are not of the world any more than I am of the world" John 17:14.), though God created us to live and prosper in this world. We are a people who live in the overlap of "in the world" and "not of this world." We are citizens of heaven, living on earth as pilgrims, "Since you call on a Father who judges each person's work impartially, live out your time as foreigners here in reverent fear" (1 Peter 1:17).

This truth did not sink into me until a few years into my immigrant experience, when I became a mother.

Motherhood and Moving

Three years into our marriage, I became pregnant. Simon and I returned to India for Ryan's birth, a choice we made to stay close to our families. Simon took up an internal assignment with his firm that allowed us to stay in India for a year.

In Indian culture, new mothers are cherished and supported. Relatives and friends filled my hospital room within hours of my giving birth. My in-laws took an overnight train from Bangalore to Hyderabad when I went into labor so they could support Simon and me and enjoy their new grandchild. There was no need to worry about food or baby supplies. Food was taken care of by a meal train organized by relatives through word of mouth. My parents and husband handled everything else.

Traditionally, the burden of caring for the mother and baby falls on the mother's family. They take over for three months. In-laws can also care for the new mom and baby, but they are not required or obliged to do so. Many Indians in the US fly their parents down from India to help with childbirth and childcare. Of course, when the child is older, both sets of parents get involved.

I went to live with my parents for three months, which is customary for most Indians. New grandparents are considered blessed by the society. The blessing comes with the responsibility of caring for the mother and baby. My mother took time off work, dedicating herself to tend to my needs and to welcome a flood of visitors, including my parents' colleagues, neighbors, and friends, who descended upon my parents' house to offer congratulations almost daily for the first few weeks. Good news, in Indian culture, is always delivered with a box of traditional sweets or desserts. The guests never left without a cup of tea and a portion of Indian sweets.

Simon and I moved into an apartment in the same city when Ryan was four months old. Neither Ryan nor I were ever alone or isolated, even when Simon worked long hours. Our neighbors were young families, too, and we quickly became friends, congregating almost every day. Friends from church visited us often. My parents came and went as often as they pleased. I also became part of a group of mothers whose babies went to a local Gymboree. Interacting with other new mothers gave me the encouragement I badly needed as a mother, as we shared stories and swapped advice on motherhood and parenting. My life was consumed with taking care of Ryan and keeping up with all my social appointments.

Shortly after Ryan turned a year old, we returned to America, to a one-bedroom apartment in Redondo Beach, California. Instantly, I missed the spaciousness of our three-bedroom home in India. The silence of our new place contrasted with the cacophony of street noises and neighbors' voices that characterized apartment living in India. The sudden disappearance of a social network made me feel as though the safety net had been pulled from underneath me. I free fell into an abyss of uncertainty.

On the surface my relationship with my husband seemed fine. But a sense of resentment brewed within me. I blamed Simon for bringing me to America. I convinced myself he was responsible for my feelings of abandonment. Discontentment with my marriage grew.

Then I hit rock bottom.

I went online to find a Bible study near me. I had been experiencing a constant pull toward God. A nagging restlessness in my soul lingered, and I was tired of ignoring it. Motherhood, combined with my short stay in India, was a temporary reprieve from my spiritual restlessness. I knew, instinctively, that immersing myself into God's Word would save me from drowning into hopelessness and depression. An intimate relationship with God was the only lifeboat available to me.

My online search for Bible study led me to a Bible Study Fellowship (BSF), an interdenominational parachurch organization that offers a structured Bible study for women, men, and children. When I arrived at the church that hosted the women's Bible study, I was surprised to see at least a hundred women gathered in the sanctuary. The volunteers who welcomed me with hugs and smiles exuded warmth and genuine joy.

I did not know what to expect, as I had never been part of a women's Bible study before. All I wanted was to be accountable about my Bible reading habits, to grow in my walk with God, and to have conversations about faith with other like-minded women. The diversity in the group impressed me. Being surrounded by women from varied ethnic backgrounds made me feel comfortable and accepted.

BSF emphasized a personal time of Bible study and offered a disciplined approach to a deeper meditation on God's Word. As I studied the book of Matthew, week after week, I fell in love with Jesus all over again. My daily quiet time was no longer quiet or uneventful. It buzzed with my heart's cries and God's whispers.

I could not contain my excitement during the weekly group discussion time, where I poured my heart out to my group members about how God was meeting my needs. Listening to other women talk about their struggles and faith confirmed to me that God was at work in our lives. He never took a break from us, even when we lacked faith or wandered away from Him.

A Fresh Perspective

As the thread of my faith got stronger, I became more joyful, mindful of what Jesus had done for me on the cross. My friendship with Jesus met my needs for acceptance, approval, and affirmation. He became my treasure, and being in His presence gave me the greatest delight and satisfaction. My parched soul had finally found the sweetest and purest form of water: living water. "Jesus stood and said in a loud voice, 'Let anyone who is thirsty come to me and drink. Whoever believes in me, as Scripture has said, rivers of living water will flow from within them'" (John 7:37–38).

Over the next few months, as I spent more time with God, my perception of my situation underwent a transformation. I saw my role as a woman, mother, wife, immigrant, and more importantly, as a child of God with a renewed mindset. I went from being bitter with my husband about moving us to a foreign country away from home, to becoming appreciative of his companionship and support. I recognized God's sovereignty in my marriage and in my husband's demanding job.

I understood that the source of tension in my marriage was misplaced affections and expectations. Simon could never meet all my needs, no matter how earnestly he tried. He could not be my husband, friend, sister, mother, and father. He could not be home and shelter. He could not be my strength and rock.

Only Jesus could be all and everything. Jesus was sufficient for me.

It was liberating and life giving to peel my eyes away from myself and fix my eyes on Jesus. Like new dew drops that appeared on blades of grass every morning, a healthy dose of gratitude filled my heart each day. I was thankful, no doubt, for my material blessings, but I was even more thankful for my identity and destiny in Jesus Christ.

My recharged enthusiasm for God flowed into my parenting. I took delight in teaching spiritual truths to Ryan and enjoyed answering his innocent questions. I viewed motherhood as a gift. My son belonged to God who had entrusted him to me. It was I who considered it a privilege to shepherd Ryan's soul and walk alongside him as he grew in his faith.

A year after we returned to the US with Ryan, our small family moved to a larger apartment in Torrance, California, less than five miles away from Redondo Beach. Though I gained new friends in the new neighborhood, I remembered that my joy was not tied to the lack or abundance of friends. My joy was attached to my friendship with Jesus.

God wanted me to bloom where He had planted me and look for opportunities to bless others with His love wherever He planted me. Maybe someone in that apartment building needed a friend. Maybe someone had to see, up close, what a Christian family looked like. Maybe someone was curious about Jesus. God had a reason for every neighborhood I lived in and every situation that caused me struggle or stress.

Surrendering my wishes and plans to God let me walk the path God chose for me. He impressed upon me the temporary and short nature of my stay on earth. When my time on earth will end, I will be home in Immanuel's land. Heaven is my destiny. My earthly life is a journey that has a purpose: to further God's kingdom and bring Him glory. This revelation infused my life with joy, meaning, and hope.

Heavenly Citizenship

Our citizenship in heaven forms a crucial aspect of our identity as Christ followers. We are not citizens of earth who put their confidence in their flesh and who desire the things of the world. Paul refers to them as "enemies of the cross of Christ" in Philippians 3:18, then he expands on their nature: "Their destiny is destruction, their god is their stomach, and their glory is in their shame. Their mind is set on earthly things" (Philippians 3:19). He contrasts citizens of earth with true believers who are citizens of heaven: "But your citizenship is in heaven" (Philippians 3:20).

As citizens of heaven, we align ourselves with heaven. We pray to our Father in heaven, asking for His will to be done "on earth as it is in heaven" (Matthew 6:9–10). Our mindset is heavenly, so we store up treasures in heaven (Matthew 6:19–21). Our conduct points others to Christ and glorifies our Father in heaven (Matthew 5:16).

This heaven-oriented identity reminds us that we owe our allegiance to Jesus the King and are called to live by the standards of God's kingdom. We can impact heaven with our radical and countercultural actions on earth.

Undivided love for God motivates believers to prioritize kingdom purposes over earthly pleasures or success. Possessions, money, power, status, fame, and other worldly charms do not appeal to a heart that is devoted to God.

Citizens of heaven are a people in transition, living between the two advents. We are a people who straddle two cultures, one that belongs to the kingdom of God and one that is of the world. We are a people who live in the "here-but-not-yet" tension because though Jesus inaugurated the kingdom of God on earth, it has not yet been fully consummated.

Embracing our identity as foreigners on earth causes us to set our hearts on Christ and inspires us to follow Him with urgency and passion. Like Paul, we can persevere in faith and live a purpose-driven life. "I press on toward the goal to win the prize for which God has called me heavenward in Christ Jesus" (Philippians 3:14).

The apostle Paul relentlessly pursued his mission to take the gospel to the ends of the earth. He planted churches and made disciples, moving from one place to the next and never calling any place on earth home. Paul worked hard, using his time and resources and every available opportunity including writing letters to edify the church, "He is the one we proclaim, admonishing and teaching everyone with all wisdom, so that we may present everyone fully mature in Christ. To this end I strenuously contend with all the energy Christ so powerfully works in me" (Colossians 1:28–29).

Everywhere Paul proclaimed the gospel, he faced opposition and rejection. He was driven out of towns, put in prisons, and tortured for Christ (2 Corinthians 11:23–27). He never wavered from his commitment in spite of enduring tremendous physical and emotional suffering. What mattered most to Paul was to do God's will and follow God's agenda, no matter the cost. The promise of future glory and eternal fellowship with Jesus gave him hope, comfort, and strength.

Paul was neither a superhero nor a perfect human being. But God used him, and other apostles and followers, to lay the foundation for the early church. Paul embraced his otherworldly identity as a citizen of heaven, not caring for earthly glamour or glitz. Paul's life and ministry had a profound impact on the early church, and he continues to amaze and inspire believers around the world by his purpose-driven and passionate life.

An Eternal Perspective

The Old Testament "heroes of faith," Abraham, Isaac, Jacob, Moses, David, and others mentioned in Hebrews 11, were immigrants who called many places home. But they were aware of their true spiritual identity as aliens on earth, wearing their foreignness as a badge of honor—"All these people were still living by faith when they died. They did not receive the things promised; they only saw them and welcomed them from a distance, admitting that they were foreigners and strangers on earth" (Hebrews 11:13).

The patriarchs' belief that they were sojourners on earth made them long "for a better country—a heavenly one" (Hebrews 11:16). They pushed through hardships and heartaches, looking forward to the fulfillment of the promises made to them by God. Their iron-clad faith caused them to look beyond their earthly trials to an inheritance preserved for them.

In direct contrast to the settlers of this world, the heroes of Hebrews 11 prioritized righteousness over the riches and pleasures of this world. They chased after God's heart rather than pursue their own happiness.

Our identity as immigrants on earth gives us an eternal perspective which directs our attention upward: "Since, then, you have been raised with Christ, set your hearts on things above, where Christ is, seated at the right hand of God. Set your minds on things above, not on earthly things" (Colossians 3:1–2). An eternal perspective keeps us focused on what matters—loving God and loving others. An eternal perspective can cause us to live so outrageously for God that we become as noticeable as a brown-skinned Indian in a crowd of white Americans, drawing attention to God and His ways.

An eternal perspective also helps us push through crises with hope. In John 16:33, Jesus warned His disciples that the road ahead would be difficult when He said, "In this world you will have trouble." They would not be exempt or protected from agony and sorrow in this world. But He assured them that they would have peace in Him, inexplicable and supernatural peace that would sustain them and steady their hearts during rough times. Because Jesus overcame the world, they, too, with the help of the Holy Spirit, could overcome suffering and sin.

We can hold on to Jesus's words when we experience adversity. He promises to be with us and not let us suffer alone. His peace and joy provide comfort and strength. Our suffering, no matter how great or small, is temporary. When Christ returns and takes us home, we can bid farewell once and for all to hardships, tears, and pain.

The apostle Paul, who suffered a great deal for the sake of Christ, urged us to look at the big picture: "For our light and momentary troubles are achieving for us an eternal glory that far outweighs them all. So we fix our eyes not on what is seen, but on what is unseen, since what is seen is temporary, but what is unseen is eternal" (2 Corinthians 4:17–18). His long-term vision transformed his view on his trials and he believed that, on the other side of eternity, he would share in Christ's glory and reign with Him. Like Paul and other apostles, we can cast our sights on the unseen and eternal: "I consider that our present sufferings are not worth comparing with the glory that will be revealed in us" (Romans 8:18).

The founders of the early church were persecuted and martyred for relentlessly preaching the gospel. They lived in a hostile world, surrounded by a culture that was immoral and idolatrous. Choosing to follow Christ was not only unpopular but also dangerous. It did not stop them, however, from dedicating their lives to the mission given to them by their Savior—to take the good news to the end of the world, *making disciples for Christ.*

They executed their mission with exigency because they were conscious of the transient and unpredictable nature of their mortal lives. Their eternal perspective enabled them to accomplish great things for God's kingdom. When crisis came knocking on their doors, they did not crumble into pieces or question their identity. Empowered by the Holy Spirit, they pressed on, like athletes in a marathon, keeping their attention on the prize.

Passion and Purpose

Knowing that we are citizens of heaven and strangers on earth can excite us and fill us with joyful hope. If our hearts are attached to Jesus, we desire nothing better than to sit at His feet, listen to Him, speak with Him, and serve Him. Sometimes, we are so burdened by our problems or so distracted by worldly affairs that we don't experience a deep desire for God. At such times, we can go to Jesus with our doubts and concerns. We can ask Him to fill our cup, and He will answer our prayers. He will honor our longing for a closer walk with Him. God will open our eyes so we will see ourselves as pilgrims on earth and members of His heavenly kingdom.

When I finally grasped what it meant to live like a spiritual immigrant, my life was transformed. I had let the challenges of my literal immigrant experience adversely affect my relationship with God and shake the foundations of my identity. I had withdrawn deeper into the valley of self-pity, caring predominantly about my comfort and security. But accepting my identity as a spiritual immigrant recalibrated my focus, steering my thoughts toward Jesus and His kingdom.

I embrace the feelings of not belonging, not being rooted, and not feeling at home. The more I love Jesus, the deeper my longing for eternal fellowship with Him. I know I belong to God's kingdom. My citizenship in heaven informs my life on earth—how I manage time, money, and relationships; how I point others to God; and how I bring glory to Him. When I experience hardships, I can hold on to the hope of heaven that is mine.

I welcome being treated as an outsider for identifying with Jesus. My immigrant identity anchors me to Jesus, the ultimate immigrant, and encourages me to imitate His eternal perspective. I hope, like Jesus, I can stay focused on my purpose on earth—to do the will of the Father, even and especially when it's hard or inconvenient or makes me stand out.

Reach In

1. When was the last time you felt like an outsider in a particular setting?

_____

2. How often do you feel out of place in this world on account of your faith in God?

_____

3. How does the promise of heaven affect your daily living?

_____

4. In what way does the understanding of your immigrant identity change how you view your current problems or challenges?

5. What is your purpose in life? How does your identity as a citizen of heaven influence your purpose?

Reach Out

Share the promise and hope of heaven with a friend who does not believe in God. Or remind a fellow believer who's facing a challenging situation about their heavenly future and encourage them to persevere in faith.

Reach Up

Dear Father in Heaven,

I thank You for granting me citizenship to Your kingdom. You loved me even before I knew You and gave Your Son up so that I can be a part of Your family and a member of Your kingdom. I believe my time is in Your hands. Walk with me on this earthly journey. Draw me closer to You. Help me see my life through an eternal lens. Turn my eyes toward You and Your purposes for me. I surrender my life to You. May Your plans be my plans. Give me courage and wisdom to tell others about Your great love for them. Thank You for preserving for me an eternal inheritance. May I never lose sight of it. Encourage me to hope in heaven when my strength fails and my fears pile up. Lift me up with Your able hands and turn my face toward Yours. Give me a distaste for the things of the world and increase my appetite for righteousness. May my sojourn on earth bring You glory, and may Your will be done on earth as it is in heaven.

Amen.

CHAPTER 5
Identity and Calling

For we are God's handiwork, created in Christ Jesus to do
good works, which God prepared in advance for us to do.

Ephesians 2:10

I had mixed feelings about volunteering at church that Friday night. I wished I had a last-minute excuse not to go.

Every Friday, I served in the children's ministry at our church in Los Angeles. Usually, I looked forward to praying with other volunteers, setting up the class, interacting with children, worshipping with them, and helping them learn about God. It was fun and rewarding. But I had had a rough week. All I wanted to do was to sit on my couch and watch TV that Friday night. I forced myself to get ready and dragged my feet to the car. As I pulled into the parking lot of the church, I prayed, *God, I'm here, though I don't want to be here. Please change my heart. Help me to serve you well today.*

I was ready to teach a Bible lesson to the fourth and fifth graders. When I got to the church, however, the supervisors informed me there was an unexpected shortage of volunteers. They sent me to assist the teacher who was teaching the second and third graders.

I complained to God. *I spent hours preparing to teach the older kids! All that hard work amounts to nothing.* I knew, however, that God had a purpose for the last-minute change. He wanted me to trust Him and follow His cues.

While I was assisting the second graders, a girl sitting in a corner with her shoulders hunched and hair covering her face caught my attention. I went over, sat next to her, and introduced myself. "Do you need help with the worksheet?"

She nodded. On one corner of the worksheet, I noticed she had scribbled the words, "I'm not good."

I pointed at the writing. "Why do you feel that way?"

She opened up to me without making eye contact. "I can't do this puzzle. I'm not good at it. I'm not good at anything."

"That's not true." I placed my hand gently on her shoulder. "God has blessed us all with special gifts and talents. Tell me about an activity or game that you're good at."

The girl stared at her worksheet. A smile slowly appeared on her face. She looked me in the eye. "I'm great at drawing."

She and I chatted for a little longer and completed the worksheet together. I wondered if she was the reason I was reassigned to this class. Before I could mull over the question, a volunteer beckoned me. "Could you please speak with the Indian lady who is seated in the waiting area?"

The staff told me she was the grandmother of one of the girls who attended the Friday evening kids' church. Her son was married to a white Christian woman. For some reason, she left the main sanctuary midservice and wanted to be near her granddaughter. Her daughter-in-law accompanied her.

I approached the waiting area and noticed an elderly lady in a *salwar-kameez*. She wore a red *bindi* on her forehead. Her face seemed strained. She looked around as if she was searching for something.

"Hello, Aunty!" I introduced myself and asked how she was doing in Hindi. I exchanged pleasantries with her daughter-in-law.

Relieved to see another Indian in church, she told me in broken Hindi that she could speak neither Hindi nor English. She understood little Hindi and could fluently speak only Gujrati. I assured her I would do my best to understand her Gujrati, a language spoken in the Western state of Gujrat in India. Her American daughter-in-law smiled hesitantly and expressed to me that her mother-in-law was feeling extremely uncomfortable in the church and that she had no idea how to put her at ease. I told her I understood. She was a conservative Hindu woman who probably had never set foot inside a church even in India. And now, she had stepped into a world that was completely foreign.

I pulled up a chair and sat with them, concentrating most of my attention on the elderly lady. We managed to communicate with each other in two different languages. The mother-in-law did most of the talking. She lived in India and was only visiting her son's family in America. We conversed until the children's church was over.

During my drive back home, I pondered the events of that morning. I thought I was going to teach a bunch of nine- and ten-year-old children. I had come close to canceling going to church. But God had different plans for that night, which included a shy second grader and an Indian woman from Gujrat. He did not want me to teach but show up and make myself available. God used me to come alongside the little girl and instill confidence in her. He wanted me to sit with and listen to an Indian lady who felt lost and alone. And my ethnicity uniquely qualified me to reach out to this lady and put her at ease. God had specific jobs planned for me that Friday evening, which were part of His larger schemes. I knew that He wanted me to put aside my plans and follow His lead.

This incident prompted me to examine my life and reflect on my struggles with finding identity and purpose. What was my purpose in life? What role did my identity play in my purpose?

While it is true that all believers share the same core spiritual identity in Christ, we each have a distinctive identity that is entwined with the plans and purposes God has for us.

Moses's Identity Struggles

Moses's life illustrates how discovering our God-given identity unlocks the power of our earthly purpose.

Moses was born to a family of Hebrew slaves in Egypt at a time when the brutality of the xenophobic Egyptian regime reached epic proportions. It was not enough to torture the Israelites with brutal, forced labor. The Pharaoh's edict to kill all male babies demonstrated the extent to which the regime went to inflict suffering on the Israelites (Exodus 1:10–16, 22) and oppress them.

In a strange twist of divinely orchestrated events, baby Moses not only lived but also was adopted by an Egyptian princess who raised him as a royal in the luxuries of the palace. He was used to comfort and excess. As a young man, Moses was probably being groomed to be the next ruler of Egypt: "Moses was educated in all the wisdom of the Egyptians and was powerful in speech and action" (Acts 7:22). He commanded respect and authority from the Egyptians and was well-known across the country and even beyond its borders as Pharaoh's son.

But Moses may not have envisioned himself as a future leader of Egypt. Because somewhere along the way, he started identifying himself with the Hebrews and saw them, and not the Egyptians, as his own people. It could have been that being brought up by his biological mother for the first few years of his childhood instilled in him a mysterious connection with the Hebrews. His identity crisis caused him to act irrationally when he saw an Egyptian beating a Hebrew slave. Moses killed the Egyptian and hid his body (Exodus 2:11–12).

Moses fled Egypt as a fugitive and a political refugee, leaving everything behind. He was around forty years of age, a grown man, with all the threads of his identity lost. In a matter of days, he went from being an important and recognized man to being a nobody.

Moses found refuge in Midian, where he had no choice but to embrace the opportunity to start with a clean slate. A former prince, he now lived the life of a shepherd, working hard to make ends meet.

With no family or community to call his own, a stranger in a foreign land, Moses found favor in the eyes of a local, Reuel, who gave his daughter, Zipporah, to him in marriage. Even though he started a family and began to lay down roots in Midian, he continued to feel like a foreigner. As if to memorialize his foreignness, he named his firstborn son, Gershom: "Zipporah gave birth to a son, and Moses named him Gershom, saying, 'I have become a foreigner in a foreign land'" (Exodus 2:22).

Another forty years passed by.

Moses's Encounter with God

When Moses settled down into his new life in Midian and probably also put to rest his identity issues, his life took another fascinating turn. He was pulled into a surreal meeting with God by a bush that was cloaked in fire but did not burn up (Exodus

3:3). As if that was not peculiar enough, Moses heard God speaking to Him directly. God's message for him was even more astounding.

He asked Moses to lead the Israelites, his people and God's chosen people, out of their bondage in Egypt. God's command would have seemed unusual and strange to Moses because he was removed from both the Israelites and the Egyptians. He would have thought of them as peoples of his past but not his present or future. Moses did not shy away from expressing his misgivings about this lofty mission: "But Moses said to God, 'Who am I that I should go to Pharaoh and bring the Israelites out of Egypt?'" (Exodus 3:11). He certainly did not think he was the most eligible candidate for the task at hand and offered up every excuse he could think of. To say that he was hesitant or scared to follow God's lead was an understatement.

Moses also had never truly known his Hebrew brothers and never faced the back-breaking oppression that they were subjected to under Pharaoh's rule. While they tarried, he had led a comfortable life in Pharaoh's palace for the first forty years of his life, and for the next forty years, he lived as a content shepherd in Midian.

Though still unsure of himself and riddled with doubts and questions, Moses showed extraordinary faith in God when He obeyed and set out to Egypt: "Now the LORD had said to Moses in Midian, 'Go back to Egypt, for all those who wanted to kill you are dead.' So, Moses took his wife and sons, put them on a donkey and started back to Egypt. And he took the staff of God in his hand" (Exodus 4:19–20). Uprooted again, Moses embarked on a journey that would make him a foreigner thrice over.

But this time, he did not leave with someone's blood on his hands. He left with God's staff in his hand.

He did not leave fearing for his safety. He left with the assurance that God was with him.

He did not leave without a plan. He left with a purpose, a goal.

He did not depart with decades of identity struggles as baggage. He departed with the surety that he was called and chosen by God to be the redeemer of the Israelites.

The Shaping of Identity

When we zoom out and examine Moses's life, we see that every situation was planned by God to lead up to this moment in his life. God orchestrated the events of his life, both in Egypt and Midian, to prepare him to lead His people not only out of slavery but also through years of wandering in the wilderness. All the unpredictable changes, difficult transitions, and seasons of suffering and struggles primed Moses for his ultimate destiny and shaped his identity.

The prophet of God went down in history neither as an Egyptian, Israelite, nor Midianite, but as a leader appointed by God to redeem His people.

God used Moses not just to rescue the Israelites but also to give them His Law and train them to step into their identity as the people of God.

When God chose Moses for the job, he was unsure of himself and shy of speech. But Moses obeyed God and stepped into his leadership appointment, believing that God would equip him.

God Gives Us Purpose

Moses's encounter with God at the burning bush reveals the reasons Moses surrendered his concerns, weaknesses, struggles, and questions to God and trusted God's plan for his life.

When God spoke to Moses, He reminded Moses, more than once, who He was. Moses was speaking with the God of his forefathers—the God of Abraham, the God of Isaac, and the God of Jacob (Exodus 3:6, 15–16; 4:5). God clarified this truth in order to leave no doubt in Moses's mind that his task was sanctioned and ordained by the God of the Hebrews and that He would take care of all details concerning this mission. God declared His identity to Moses loud and clear, "I AM WHO I AM. This is what you are to say to the Israelites: I AM has sent you" (Exodus 3:14). Generations had passed, but Israel's God remained immutable. He fully intended to keep His covenant with Israel. Moses could put his trust in God because His track record of faithfulness was unparalleled.

Though Moses hesitated at first, God matured his faith one step at a time. The plagues, the parting of the Red Sea, and countless other miracles demonstrate what a powerful messenger of God Moses had become.

Moses's story teaches us that trying to find our true identity outside of God is an exercise in futility. Nobody knows us better than our Creator. Any identity we create on our own is no more than an avatar—unreal, temporal, and fragile. However, when we commit our search for identity to God, He reveals His identity and His purpose.

Identity and calling are two sides of the same coin. Moses had to confront challenges stemming from his ethnic and cultural identity. But when he found his purpose in life, he stepped into his identity as the God-appointed prophet and leader of the Israelites. His ethnic identity, though important to the narrative, faded in the background. His mission confirmed his spiritual identity.

Other biblical characters also became agents of God's work because they were secure in their identity and calling. In the New Testament, we read stories of the fishermen who became apostles and martyrs of the faith, leaving their nets when Jesus called them to become His disciples. They had no idea where their new career path would take them. Jesus promised to make them fishers of men. Jesus's twelve disciples went on to change the world!

Our Unique Purpose

As followers of Jesus, we share the same calling. We are all created for His pleasure and glory (Revelation 4:11). We are agents of change in this world, called to proclaim Christ through our lives (Matthew 28:19–20). The purpose of our pilgrim journey on earth is to be messengers of God's truth to a world that is lost and dying (2 Corinthians 5:20–21). We are called to lay down our lives for others, just like Jesus did (1 John 3:16). We are called to bring Him glory through everything we do (Isaiah 43:7). This is the grand plan for our pilgrimage. Our perspective as citizens of heaven is key to helping us fix our eyes on our calling, God's plan for us.

Even though all believers share a common goal, the way we are called to execute our purposes is unique. Our assignments are created and tailored just for us. God has an exclusive plan designed specifically for every single one of us. He uses the completely distinctive combination of our upbringing, cultural background, nationality, education, professional experiences, spiritual gifts, natural talents, and even trials to tailor a unique path and purpose for our lives.

God does not reveal His purpose all at once. The more we walk in His ways, the clearer the plan gets. It is unwrapped, slowly and steadily, like a precious gift. Living for God, faithfully and obediently, day by day, is the best thing we can do to find our way into the identity and calling He has handcrafted for us. God's purposes for us change with the seasons of our lives. It is possible that for several years, all that God requires from us is to be faithful in the mundane duties of our lives. A wise and discerning believer will see these seasons as periods of preparation and training.

One of those seasons in my life was when I became a mother. As a new stay-at-home mom, I remember feeling frustrated with sleeplessness and tiredness. I grumbled about the hardship of caring for a baby. The good Father made me see the error of my ways and wanted me to serve Him joyfully, not grudgingly, by being a loving mother to the son He gave me, the son who was His, not mine to begin with. I found it boring to talk to a toddler who never talked back to me, let alone understand what I said. I spent my days obsessing over my son's sleep and potty schedules.

But the joy of motherhood included the mess of dirty diapers and complicated baby carriers. Whenever I felt physically exhausted or mentally drained, I reminded myself that, at this point in my life, God's plan for me was to devote myself to care for my baby boy. The Holy Spirit helped me find satisfaction and joy in embracing my identity and calling as a mother. And He also impressed upon me that my God-given responsibility was to lay a solid biblical foundation for the identity of my son.

Our Identity, a Privilege

No doubt the initial years of my immigrant experience brought anguish and tears, but I'm grateful for the challenges I faced as an immigrant. They triggered an identity crisis that was unsettling and disorienting, but they led me to discover who I really was—a citizen of heaven. I was a citizen of heaven when I was living a deeply rooted life in India, and I'm a citizen of heaven now while I make my home in America. My identity in Christ remains the same irrespective of my geographic location, race, age, health condition, or marital status.

God's purposes for me, however, can change depending on the stage of my life and the level of spiritual maturity. When I was a young girl, I envied people who knew exactly what they wanted to be when they grew up. Their gifts could be easily identified. I, on the other hand, was never sure of what I wanted to become. At one point, I wanted to be an oceanographer, but I changed my mind. I graduated from college with a degree in mathematics and computer science, but I had no interest in pursuing a career in either field. I wanted to be a French translator, having studied the language in college and fallen in love with it. But I went on to pursue an MBA in human resources and marketing and held jobs in various management positions after completing my MBA. I used to be a private French tutor on the side.

All along, my inability to pinpoint my purpose with precision frustrated me and contributed to many a sleepless night. I often thought, *what is wrong with me?*

My involvement with the church spanned various ministries. For a period of five years, I served my church in India as the leader of the youth dance and choreography team. I also taught Sunday school briefly, both in India as well as in the US. Now, I'm a writer and speaker. I love ministering to women by facilitating Bible studies and teaching God's Word. I'm also pursuing a masters in theological studies.

God has taught me that I cannot look for purpose and calling in roles, careers, and occupations. The overarching purpose of my sojourn is to live for God and for His glory.

Jesus is my King, and my allegiance to Him takes precedence not only over my allegiance to any other country but also over any claim I have over my own life. Jesus purchased my life with

His blood. I submit to His lordship. I surrender to His authority. I live by His laws. I am not the lord of my life . . . He is. My relationship with Jesus is the basis on which my identity and purpose stand.

I'm humbled to think that God would associate Himself and His identity with a frail, fragile, and flawed mortal like me. Who am I that God would want to select and appoint me for His amazing purposes? The fact that He has chosen me to be His child makes me wake up every morning with joy deep inside. I do not always see much of the road ahead nor am I sure of where He wants to take me and what He ultimately has in store for me.

But I know who I am in Christ, and that knowledge is sufficient for me to live every day in His power, trusting Him every step of the way. I can be confident that He will unravel His fantastic plan for me as I walk in obedience to Him. By being faithful to the day-to-day tasks He has put in front of me, I can prepare myself to take bigger and bolder steps for Him.

Reach In

1. Reflecting back on the events of your life, how do you see God's hand at work in shaping your identity and calling?

2. What steps are you taking daily to seek God's will for your life?

3. Are you resisting God's call to serve Him in any area of your life? If yes, what fears and doubts are keeping you from obeying God?

4. Recollect a difficult time in your recent past. Can you identify God's purpose for your suffering?

Reach Out

Do you know anyone who is wrestling with questions about identity and calling? Talk with them about your identity in Christ and how it gives your life meaning.

Reach Up

Dear Father in Heaven,

I praise You because You are a good, loving Father. I trust in Your promises and providence. Thank You for being with me every day of my life. Thank You for providing for me and protecting me through all the bad times in my life. Thank You for using both challenges and blessings to mold my identity. May I desire to do Your will, not mine. Equip me to carry out Your plans for me. I surrender to You my weaknesses and failings. Give me Your grace and strength. Help me to obey You as You direct my steps. May everything I do, think, and say bring glory and honor to Your name.

Amen.

CHAPTER 6
Strangers on Earth

*Jesus said, "My kingdom is not of this world.
If it were, my servants would fight to prevent my arrest
by the Jewish leaders.
But now my kingdom is from another place."*

John 18:36

"Did you try Froot Loops?" my friend asked.

"What do Froot Loops have to do with potty training?" I was perplexed. She and I were chatting about our kids one Sunday morning after church. I shared my frustrations about toilet training my three-year-old son.

"Put some of the colorful cereal in the toilet and teach your son to 'aim and fire'." She smiled.

My body stiffened and my eyes grew wide while I managed to smile back. Was she actually suggesting I throw food down the toilet? I changed the topic after I recovered from the shock.

While it may be perfectly acceptable to Americans to use food for reasons other than eating, it is akin to a crime to most Indians to waste food or use it for nonedible reasons. I could not take my friend's suggestion as it went against my cultural sensibilities.

The contrast in Indian and American cultures became more apparent in the area of parenting than in any other aspect of my life. A separate nursery for a newborn baby does not exist in India. Cosleeping is the norm for most Indians. Children often do not get their own rooms until they are eight or ten years old. The thought that children need privacy is inconceivable. Independence is not a value that is highly prized by Indian society. Little ones and young adults alike are deliberately trained into an interdependent relationship with their parents. Contrary to the philosophy of parenting in the West, children are not expected to leave the nest and detach themselves from their parents at the age of eighteen. And children are expected to provide that support and care for their parents when they get older.

I realized that as an immigrant parent, I had a lot of unlearning and learning to do. I have been implanted with parenting wisdom that has been passed on to me from generation to generation. But I am raising my son in another culture, and most of my inherent parenting philosophies do not seem to make sense in America.

Parenting in a foreign culture has made me somewhat of an expert at negotiating cultures. Whether I'm conscious of it or not, there's a war of voices inside my head that pulls me in different directions. It goes well beyond Froot Loops. Views on dating and marriage. Modes of discipline. Posture toward elders. Which aspects of my Indian parenting wisdom do I let go of? Which American parenting norms do I adopt? I'm constantly evaluating and analyzing the benefits and costs of giving and taking between two cultures.

The result is that I've landed on a parenting style that's a mix of Indian and American mores. Unlike many Indians, we gave Ryan his own room but not until he turned four. My son is allowed to call most American adults by their first name, but he has been taught to prefix an Aunty or Uncle to the first name before addressing an Indian adult. Ryan knows more about cricket, a sport popular in India and other Commonwealth countries, than American football or baseball. While Simon and I do not believe that eighteen is a magic age at which every child transforms into a mature adult, we want to raise him to be a responsible and independent citizen. Unlike Indian teenagers who do not work while they are in school, we expect Ryan to have a summer job and earn money to pay for his own hobbies or outings.

Sometimes, this unique parenting style tends to make me feel all the more foreign. It also reinforces the fact that I live between two cultures.

Culture clashes are integral not only to my identity as an Indian

American immigrant but also to my amphibious identity as a citizen of heaven and resident alien on earth.

Two Cultures

Christians live in between two opposing cultures. The biblical values that inform our lifestyles as citizens of God's kingdom are incompatible with the secular values espoused by the world. Kingdom culture values humility, servant-leadership, and dependence on God while the world treats the humble as weak, believes leaders should be served, and promotes self-reliance and self-sufficiency. We are foreigners on earth because we swim against the tide of the dominant culture.

The Sermon on the Mount lays out a vision of God's kingdom. Its citizens are meek, merciful, pure, and poor in spirit. We rejoice in persecution and find purpose in suffering rather than look for ways to escape pain at all costs, seeking comfort and pleasure. Forgiveness, not revenge, and generosity, not greed, are the characteristics of a faithful Christian.

Jesus's followers love Him with all their heart, soul, and mind—nothing less. We give Him our whole lives, not holding back anything, because we acknowledge we are unworthy recipients of His lavish grace and love, not forgetting for a moment that Jesus purchased us with His blood.

A natural by-product of the Christian life is that we will attract the ire of unbelievers, just like Jesus warned, "If the world hates you, keep in mind that it hated me first. If you belonged to the world, it would love you as its own. As it is, you do not belong to the world, but I have chosen you out of the world. That is why the world hates you" (John 15:18–19).

Nowadays, Christians seem to be viewed more and more with disdain and ridicule. Christian ideals are often scoffed at and considered old-fashioned or narrow minded. Christ followers are becoming an unpopular minority because the world views us as a threat to the flourishing of their culture.

Amidst an increasingly hostile landscape, believers are called to fearlessly live out their identity as aliens and not shy away from standing up for what and who they represent. Fortunately, the Bible is replete with examples of men and women who took a bold stand for God. Examining their lives can embolden and encourage us to do the same.

Daniel and His Friends

Daniel and his friends, Hananiah, Mishael, and Azariah were young Hebrew men taken captive to Babylon, a foreign land. Selected to undergo training to enter the king's service along with some other men, they would be groomed in matters of Babylonian law and literature for three years to prepare them for leadership positions in Babylon.

Daniel requested that his friends and he be exempt from eating the royal food and wine offered to the trainees (Daniel 1:8). Maybe the food was offered to idols. Maybe the meat was not prepared in accordance with Mosaic law. The Bible does not say. But it highlights the fact that these young men who came from royal Israelite families could not defile themselves by violating the laws of their God.

Though they were introduced to a foreign culture and immersed in the education of foreign laws, they resolved to speak up when they thought their religious identity was being compromised. Allegiance to God overruled their allegiance to any other kingdom. Daniel's conviction gave him the courage to risk favor from the officials and a comfortable future in their new homeland. The four men were captives in a foreign land, who were not being treated poorly. Rather, Babylon was investing in them and providing opportunities for a bright future. However, these men risked it all for the sake of their beliefs.

God honored their bravery and blessed their obedience. He gave them "knowledge and understanding of all kinds of literature and learning" (Daniel 1:17). At the end of their training period, the king found them to be exceptional, "The king talked with them, and he found none equal to Daniel, Hananiah, Mishael and Azariah; so they entered the king's service. In every matter of wisdom and understanding about which the king questioned them, he found them ten times better than all the magicians and enchanters in his whole kingdom" (Daniel 1:19–20).

Daniel and his friends were given new names—Belteshazzar, Shadrach, Meshach, and Abednego. Their identity was being overhauled by a new culture, kingdom, and profession. Outwardly, they were being shaped into Babylonian officers. At the core, however, they identified with the God of their forefathers. The brave men set their eyes on pleasing God, not an earthly king. God prospered them and they rose to prominence in the Babylonian administration.

Not long after this incident, the young Hebrew men were presented with another situation that compelled them to choose between their loyalty to God and the king. Nebuchadnezzar built and erected an imposing, ninety-foot-high golden idol and ordered all the officials and important men of his empire to attend its dedication. This move was both a political and a religious one meant to unify the Babylonian empire and establish Nebuchadnezzar as the ultimate sovereign power.

At the dedication ceremony, all the gathered officials were required to fall down and worship the image upon hearing the sounds of musical instruments. The punishment for disobeying the edict was death by fire. The severity of the consequence symbolized the importance of compliance with the king's command. Adherence to the command indicated that the officials recognized and submitted to Nebuchadnezzar's political and religious authority.

Shadrach, Meshach, and Abednego refused and infuriated the king with their explanation, "King Nebuchadnezzar, we do not need to defend ourselves before you in this matter. If we are thrown into the blazing furnace, the God we serve is able to deliver us from it, and he will deliver us from Your Majesty's hand. But even if he does not, we want you to know, Your Majesty, that we will not serve your gods or worship the image of gold you have set up" (Daniel 3:16–18).

Their statement exhibits their brazen devotion to God and belief in His sovereignty. The three men were willing to die rather than bow before an idol.

Nebuchadnezzar raised the heat of the furnace and threw Shadrach, Meshach, and Abednego into the furnace, hoping to make a public spectacle of their rebellion. But he was shocked to see the bound men loose and walking around in the furnace, unharmed by the flames. There was also a fourth man with them, who many scholars believe was probably the preincarnate Christ.

When the three brave men came out, they bore no signs of being in a fiery furnace (Daniel 3:27). This incident brought glory to God and signaled to a foreign people that the God of the Jews was the One True God. He was greater than any other earthly king or idol. He alone was worthy of worship.

Living in a foreign culture did not dilute the faith of these courageous men. Though they lived in Babylon, they belonged to a different kingdom.

Culture Clashes

Our culture worships all kinds of idols—materialism, politics, knowledge and learning, health and wellness, beauty, and money. We can bow down to these idols, or we can resolve to submit our lives to God. We can allow cultural idols to dictate our choices, or we can base our decisions on God's Word. Chasing worldly idols will empty us of joy and strip us of satisfaction and meaning. Created to be in union with Christ, only an intimate relationship with Him can bring contentment and meaning. Our love for Jesus will make us stand out since it contradicts a world where people love themselves, wanting to be masters of their own destinies.

There will be consequences for being conspicuous. Our friends might ignore us, mock us, or abandon us. We might even lose our jobs and incur financial losses. But, like Shadrach, Meshach, and Abednego, we can trust God to take care of the repercussions. God may not deliver us in the way we want, but He is in control, and He will reward us for choosing Him. He takes delight in us when we manifest faithfulness, courage, and obedience.

Culture clashes can sometimes wear us down. When we feel dejected, confused, or frustrated, we can remember that God is committed to growing and guarding our faith (Philippians 2:12–13,

1 Corinthians 1:8–9). We do not have to strive on our own. The Advocate, the Holy Spirit, gives us discernment and helps us obey God (John 14:26). We will make mistakes and fail God—again and again. But His grace is sufficient for us, and His power is made perfect in our weaknesses (2 Corinthians 12:9).

We are not ordinary people but citizens of God's kingdom, with access to heavenly riches and resources: "Praise be to the God and Father of our Lord Jesus Christ, who has blessed us in the heavenly realms with every spiritual blessing in Christ" (Ephesians 1:3). In Christ and with Christ, we are seated in the heavenly realms (Ephesians 2:5–6). That is the extraordinary spiritual position and place from which we carry out our pilgrimage on earth. That is the vantage point from which we overcome worldly ways. God has perfectly equipped us to live in between cultures.

Our citizenship and privilege are not, however, a call to exclusivity. Rather, our citizenship is a call to engagement and empathy. It is not God's intention that we withdraw from the world and live ascetic lives. Nor is it His will that we live in hostility toward others who do not share our citizenship. Self-righteousness and arrogance are antithetical to the Christian life.

Unless we lovingly engage with culture, we cannot carry out the plans God has for us and for the world. True, believers are God's handiwork because He gave us a new life. But we are "created in Christ Jesus to do good works" (Ephesians 2:10). The Bible urges us to live such extraordinary lives that unbelievers will be drawn to glorify God when they consider our actions, even if they heap accusations or insults on us (1 Peter 2:11–12).

Daniel's Example

Consider the life of Daniel, a Hebrew exile who became an influential leader in the foreign nation of Babylon. As his prominence grew— "Now Daniel so distinguished himself among the administrators and the satraps by his exceptional qualities that the king planned to set him over the whole kingdom" (Daniel 6:3)— his jealous counterparts looked for something corrupt in him to bring him down.

Because they did not find any grounds for charging him with wrongdoing, they went after his faith. They manipulated King Darius to institute a law which stated that anyone caught praying to anyone else but the king during the next thirty days would be thrown into the lions' den.

Daniel did not respond to this edict by giving up his daily practice of praying three times a day. Just like his friends had done years before, Daniel rebelled against the ruler of the kingdom when the laws violated his faith: "He went home to his upstairs room where the windows opened toward Jerusalem. Three times a day he got down on his knees and prayed, giving thanks to his God, just as he had done before" (Daniel 6:10).

Daniel knew that breaking the law meant he would be torn apart by savage beasts. Even if for some reason he survived the punishment, he risked his political career, status, reputation, and wealth. But none of that mattered to Daniel since his faith was more important and valuable than wealth and power.

The distraught king reluctantly ordered Daniel to be thrown into the den of lions. The next morning the king was astounded and overjoyed to learn that Daniel was unharmed. Daniel was quick to give all credit to God, "My God sent his angel, and he shut the mouths of the lions. They have not hurt me, because I was found innocent in his sight. Nor have I ever done any wrong before you, Your Majesty" (Daniel 6:22).

This incident led to Darius issuing a decree that all the people of his kingdom must fear and revere Daniel's God, the living God, whose kingdom and dominion were indestructible and eternal.

Daniel was taken captive as a teenager, and many scholars believe he was about eighty years old at the time of this event. For a span of six decades, he remained faithful to the God of his forefathers. He made no attempt to hide his religious identity or convictions in an alien land. When his values clashed with those of the land, he courageously took a stand and chose to obey God, willing to endure any punishment that came his way. He stood out in Babylon not only on account of his ethnicity and his high position but also due to his unswerving commitment to God.

Standing Out

I am an ethnic minority in my adopted country, America. I was a minority even in my homeland, India, where more than 80 percent of the population practices Hinduism and Christians constitute about 5 percent. My upbringing in India proved to be a training ground in living as an outsider.

Yet, I wondered if I was a misfit for the right reasons—for holding on to Christian ideals in the face of opposition, for exuding joy in the midst of suffering, and for showing kindness to the undeserving. I want my lifestyle to be so peculiar that unbelievers would recognize that something about me was unusual.

As an immigrant in America, I try to adapt myself to the American way of living, without losing my core Indian values. Assimilation is a slow and complex process, which results from negotiating two cultures. While I cannot give up certain Indian ideals that I cherish, I also embrace several aspects of the American culture that appeal to me or suit me.

I write thank-you notes when I receive gifts or kind gestures, I drink water with ice, and I consume coffee in oversized cups. I've adopted Thanksgiving Day with all its trimmings and stuffing as a family tradition. All of these are acquired behaviors foreign to most Indians.

The war of cultures is an integral part of my immigrant identity. But it is less important than the clash of cultures that is characteristic to my identity as a spiritual immigrant. My goal is not to become less Indian or more American. I want less of me and more of God. I want to be more like Jesus.

I'm learning to sift cultural messages through the standards of God's kingdom, whether the source of these messages lies within the Indian or American culture. As a parent, God calls me to raise my son to be a godly man who loves and fears God. His ethnic identity is important as it is God-given and God-approved. I would like my son to know his cultural roots and be proud of his heritage. But more than that, my desire is to see him embrace his identity in Christ and live out his faith boldly in a secular world.

Like Daniel and his fellow exiles, we are called to be servants of God in a culture that is antithetical to Christian values. We are called not to conform to the patterns of this world. We cannot live like the locals who do not know or love God. As we move from sinner to saved, we unlearn the ways of the world and practice the ways of God's kingdom. The Holy Spirit infuses us with zeal to hold fast to the culture of God's kingdom. He motivates us to submit to God's authority and please Him. He equips us to guard our hearts against the things of the world.

Our courageous passion to live for God's plans and purposes makes us stand out. But we embrace our identity as foreigners and press on, undeterred by the consequences, since we know that rejection and opposition are imminent and temporary. After suffering comes eternal glory and redemption: "And the God of all grace, who called you to his eternal glory in Christ, after you have suffered a little while, will himself restore you and make you strong, firm and steadfast" (1 Peter 5:10). We can rejoice in persecution, considering ourselves privileged to be identified with Christ, who Himself was a migrant to earth from a superior world: "For I have come down from heaven not to do my will but to do the will of him who sent me" (John 6:38).

A Christian's identity is not rooted in this world, yet it is God's will that we live on earth, all the while looking up to God and looking ahead to heaven. The complexity of living between two worlds gives us opportunities to connect the mundane with the supernatural in a way that glorifies Him. The dual nature of our sojourn allows us the privilege to participate in God's designs and experience union and intimacy with Christ.

Reach In

1. In what ways is your lifestyle different from your unbelieving friends?

2. Can you recall a time when you were put in a situation that challenged your faith? How were you blessed for standing up for your beliefs?

3. How can you pray for courage to obey God in the face of opposition?

4. What have you lost and what have you gained for holding fast to the culture of God's kingdom?

Reach Out

Pray for specific people who have mistreated you or falsely accused you because of your faith.

Reach Up

Dear Father in Heaven,

I thank You for giving me a new life and a new identity. Like Your Son, I, too, am not of this world. I ask for strength to stand up for You and Your kingdom in this hostile world. Help me to challenge the ways of the world that lead to sin and destruction with love and truth. Empower me to hold on to the values of the Your kingdom. Help me not to get discouraged when I'm persecuted for obeying Your commands. Strengthen my faith so that I do not fear rejection or ridicule. May I set my heart on pleasing You in everything I do. Increase my love for You so that my love for earthly things decreases. Give me wisdom so I can engage with the world without losing my unique identity. Give me opportunities so I can tell people about Your love.

Amen.

Section Two
Home

CHAPTER 7
Homeless on Earth

*Jesus replied, "Anyone who loves me will obey my
teaching. My Father will love them, and we will come
to them and make our home with them."*

John 14:23

I slouched in the couch of our living room in Southern California
and browsed photos on my sister's Facebook page from my cell
phone. The pictures were taken at one of my favorite cafes in my
hometown, Hyderabad, India—the same cafe where I used to hang
out with my friends many years ago.

The overcast day fueled my nostalgia. I missed my friends. I
missed the smell of Indian coffee. I missed giggling with my sister.

"I miss home," I muttered.

Ryan, who was immersed in the world of little building bricks,
frowned and shifted his attention from his Legos to me. I had
assumed nothing could distract him from his project. But the three
little words caught his attention. He looked up at me with a half-
built Lego train in his hands. Questions danced in his eyes.

"What do you mean, Mommy? This *is* home."

He was right. As memories from India flooded my mind, I
was knee-deep in waters of homesickness. I managed to smile back
at him, wishing I could explain my dilemma to this innocent six-
year-old child.

"I meant India, Ryan." I sighed.

When I saw comprehension slowly creep over his eyes, I added,
"This is our home. But I was born and raised in India. So, I call
India home too."

He nodded and turned his attention back to the unfinished
brick train.

I blinked, surprised that my explanation seemed to make perfect sense to him while at the same time plunged me into confusion, as my mind began to unpack the words I had just uttered.

I am an immigrant who has called many places home. The place we were living in at the time—a charming three-bedroom house in the suburbs of Los Angeles, with five varieties of roses in the garden and an antique swing in the backyard—was simultaneously home and not home.

How I wished I could explain to my six-year-old son that it was as much perplexing as it was sad that I was missing home while I was at home!

When did my view of home become so complicated?

The Basics of Home

My idea of home used to be simple. Clearly defined.

When I was a young girl, my drawing of a house consisted of a slanted roof, door, windows, chimney, a family, and a dog. I believed, then, *home* was the synthesis of a physical house with indestructible walls, an impenetrable roof, and a happy family bound together by love and loyalty.

In emigrating from the East to the West, as I was uprooted from one country and grafted into another, my image of home became distorted. My circumstances and experiences infected my emotional and spiritual world and played havoc with my construct of home.

Over and over, I confronted the same questions—*Where is my home? What is home, anyway?*

We all have our own definitions and ideas of home. Home can denote the place where we were born and raised, where we live, or where our family lives. It can be an apartment building, acres of ranch land, or a large city. Home can be defined by the people that it represents—family and friends. But home is more than physical places and real people.

Home represents an emotional space—a shelter, a shield from the chaos and confusion of a changing world. A place to feel welcome, not judged or measured by anything or anyone. A place where we can be ourselves without worrying about conforming or breaking any rules—here, if rules are meant to be broken, then brokenness is in turn meant to be accepted and forgiven.

Home is the heart of all things familiar. More than walls, carpets, furniture, and appliances. It's the smells in the kitchen. The warmth of a favorite blanket. The comfort of the couch. The familiar noise of traffic on the street outside. The welcome bark of a dog. The laughter and chatter of loved ones. The habits and customs shared over years and years.

Home is where the mind, if not the body, comes to rest at the end of a long day.

Home, in a million different ways, is an extension of us—our private possessions, our intimate feelings, the melting pot of our old and infant memories, our choices, our values, our personalities, and our identity. Consciously or not, we leave our fingerprints and footprints, both literally and figuratively, all over our homes.

It is difficult to imagine life without a home. Our inherent need for safety, security, stability, and rest makes the desire for home an indelible characteristic of the human psyche. Home is so important to most of us that we spend our lives trying to preserve, sustain, and nourish our homes. Even if we lose a home, we quickly embark upon the process of finding another home and resettling.

Setting Up a Home

My quandary about home began more than a decade ago when I tied the knot. I had lived with my parents until I was married, as was customary in Indian families. So, setting up a home with my husband was a milestone that I looked forward to with great excitement.

Simon and I visited more than twenty apartment buildings in Hyderabad before we found the one we liked. We wanted our first home to be perfect, so we threw ourselves into beautifying it. We explored nearly all the furniture shops in the city to find the best deals on every piece of furniture. We debated over the placement of the couch, the size of the TV, the color of the curtains, the necessity of a shoe cabinet, and the merits of storage compartments under the master bed.

The project of setting up and embellishing a house was painstaking but immensely gratifying. We were overjoyed with the outcome of our labor and teamwork. Our nest represented us, a fascinating melding of our own individual and shared preferences and aspirations, our curated identities and personalities.

It was important that our home represented a safe space not only to us but also to the friends and family who visited us. Hospitality was a virtue that both Simon and I valued. The doors of our house were open to friends who wanted to vent about an angry boss, relax after a difficult day, or talk about a book they read.

My husband and I settled into a routine and rhythm that suited our work lives and social outings. Day by day, our new life together and our new home started to feel familiar and right.

But not for long.

Not even three months after our wedding day, Simon was assigned a consulting project in California. The couch had barely been broken in. Our custom-made bookshelves were just installed and still smelled of wood. The roses on our balcony had finally started to bloom.

And we had to leave everything behind. We packed our bags and left our brand-new home to make another one, this time in a new country.

My husband and I found ourselves in a fully furnished, ocean-view apartment in a beach town south of Los Angeles, Redondo Beach. This was the first time we ever lived in a furnished apartment. Because nothing in the apartment belonged to us, it carried an air of impersonality despite our best efforts to infuse ourselves into it. Compared to the home we had left behind, this apartment felt detached and foreign.

But we were completely and utterly in love with each other. All that mattered was that we were together. Every other inconvenience could be overlooked. Little did we know that we would spend the next three years on the move, picking up and moving from city to city for every new work assignment, living from furnished apartment to furnished apartment across the country.

Los Angeles, Dallas, Jersey City, Morristown, Little Rock. Find a home, unpack, settle in, find friends, learn life, then pack up, say goodbyes, move to the next location.

Friends who visited us in any of our homes during this time would occasionally comment that our apartment resembled a hotel room. They were not exaggerating. The corporate furnishings created a familiar set décor. Any personal touches that we added—family pictures, sofa cushions, and artifacts from India—were superficial. I'm not sure if it was a subconscious or deliberate attempt on my part, but I developed little attachment to these homes or any of the articles in them.

We also were hesitant to make friends and build strong relationships. Simon and I were always conscious of the temporary nature of our stay.

After about four years of hopping around from place to place and being in a constant state of transition, Simon was permanently transferred to his company's Los Angeles office. I was thrilled, especially since we had just become new parents of a baby boy. I needed stability. We could finally settle down in one place and build a home. Our home. No corporate, furnished apartment this time.

We embarked upon setting up a home. Again.

Changing Definitions of Home

We spent weeks scouting houses and hours choosing the perfect media console. We researched mattress options and children's furniture. At last, we could live in a home that was our own, with our own bed, towels, coffee maker, pots, and pans. We settled on a two-bedroom apartment in Torrance, California, only ten minutes away from Redondo Beach. It was still a rented unit, but at least the stuff inside was ours. Our apartment was not furnished according to the standards of a corporate organization. Rather, it had its own character and flavor. Almost like a unique fingerprint.

As time went by, I settled down into my new lifestyle. I made new friends. I became more and more acquainted with American values, holidays, and traditions. I found a good church to call home too. I thought that I had finally reached the end of my wandering. It was all going to be good from here.

But deep inside, I faced a more fundamental conflict. I was becoming aware of a growing and persistent feeling of not belonging anywhere. Resettling was not as fluid as I had imagined. It was cumbersome and confusing. Home felt intricately tied to my identity, and it was being built up and eroded at the same time.

Trying to pin the idea of home to a physical and tangible place was evidently difficult for an immigrant like me. To define home by houses, cities, or countries no longer proved sufficient or satisfactory. So, I expanded my definition. I decided that home meant people and relationships—marriages, families, and communities.

In my early years of marriage, home meant a strong marriage. My relationship with my husband was the only stable and unchanging factor in my life. I had left everything and everyone else in a land far, far away. But I felt at home when I was in my husband's company. The surroundings melted away and became unimportant. Our marriage was our home. Our love for each other transformed every impersonal, furnished apartment and every unfamiliar culture into home sweet home. And when we had my son, our young family became the center of our lives. We built our home around him.

Ask anyone that has moved a lot, and they will tell you that home is all about the people, not the houses or the cities. The opposite is also true. We can feel alienated, unwelcome, or lost in a gathering of familiar people.

But our imagination of home may be incomplete if we base our definition on people. Sometimes, relationships can evolve or crumble. We could be crushed and feel homeless if we lose someone important or if a loved one abandons us. There has to be something more to home.

At Home with God

The stress of migration and assimilation and my search for home took me to the throne of God, again and again, for help and guidance and to simply vent. I took my questions and lament to Him. Who else could I go to? I was taught from my childhood to run to God for comfort and counsel. I knew no other way to respond to a crisis. I pleaded with my Father to help me put down roots and feel settled.

For all my confusion, this much was true—the more time I spent with Him, the more my concerns faded away into the background. Being in His presence satisfied me. My laundry list of problems, requests, and challenges sunk to the bottom of my heart, and His love, grace, and faithfulness floated to the top. Studying the Bible rekindled in me a passion for God's presence. I craved His company.

What I failed to do with my human mind and efforts, He managed to accomplish for me—He made me feel at home.

It mattered less and less where I lived or belonged when spiritually, I found shelter, permanence, and peace in God. Intimate fellowship with God is home. No other place or person can satisfy completely my need to be rooted because I am made in His image, imprinted with a desire to cohabit with Him. The human soul can feel completely at home only when it is entwined with God's Spirit, intimately and wholly.

Our home with God should be the only secure and permanent home that can fully satisfy us.

It was an extraordinarily enlightening journey for me that I could actually find a secure home here on earth, even as I look forward to my perfect and permanent home on the other side of eternity!

I was eager to unpack the lives of biblical characters who were immigrants like me, to learn how their approach to the idea of home could help transform my own practical devotion to God.

Abraham's Faith

Venerated as a hero of faith, Abraham is one of the most important characters in the Bible. He played a crucial role in God's grand story of the redemption of mankind. God chose Abraham to become the founding father of the nation of Israel. He initiated and drafted His covenant with His people, the Israelites, through him. And God called Abraham when he was older (some scholars estimate he may have been at least seventy-five years old) and well-settled.

A native of Ur, Abraham belonged to a wealthy and influential family. When God asked Abraham to leave his home, He didn't even reveal to him the final destination. Still, Abraham obeyed God and left Harran, a place where he had put down roots: "He took his wife Sarai, his nephew Lot, all the possessions they had accumulated and the people they had acquired in Harran, and they set out for the land of Canaan, and they arrived there" (Genesis 12:5).

It would not have been easy for Abraham to leave his country, his community, and his people and move to an unknown place where he would be a stranger. He may not have left joyfully, but he left with hope and confidence in God's plans for him.

God promised to bless Abraham and make him into a great nation:

> I will make you into a great nation,
>   and I will bless you;
> I will make your name great,
>   and you will be a blessing.
> I will bless those who bless you,
>   and whoever curses you I will curse;
> and all peoples on earth
>   will be blessed through you.
>   (Genesis 12:2–3)

The patriarch took God's promises to heart and followed God's leading.

Abraham willingly uprooted himself and became an immigrant. He completely relied on God to be his compass, his map, and his guide. His faith in God was greater than the sum of his fears and reservations. The Bible does not suggest that his circumstances made migration favorable. He was not fleeing to find safety. He was not leaving for better economic opportunities. In fact, the opposite seemed to be true—he had no reason to migrate but for the command of God.

Throughout his life, Abraham didn't just move once, but again and again at God's command. His unwavering faith illustrates that he was not attached to his earthly homes or things. He considered his relationship with God to be more precious than anything else. The patriarch's sense of security and self-worth was not located in possessions, places, or even people. He was willing to even sacrifice his only son, Isaac, upon God's command (Genesis 22:1–18).

Abraham's life foreshadowed the journey of his descendants, the people of Israel, toward the promised land. Even further, his sojourning life is a model for the believer's passage through this earthly existence.

Abraham lived as a stranger on earth, holding on loosely to his earthly homes and belongings while fixing his eyes on heaven, his future home: "By faith he made his home in the promised land like a stranger in a foreign country; he lived in tents, as did Isaac and Jacob, who were heirs with him of the same promise. For he was looking forward to the city with foundations, whose architect and builder is God" (Hebrews 11:9–10). He was conscious of the transient nature of his life and the permanence of his friendship with God.

Abraham's strong grasp on his identity as an immigrant informed his concept of home. He made a home on earth with God's presence and promises. Nothing mattered to him more than to dwell with God.

Like Abraham, David too anchored his faith and hope not in a stable, earthly home but in God.

David's Home

David, a young shepherd, was chosen by God to become the next king of Israel while Saul was still on the throne. His military conquests made Saul jealous. David was on the run for most of his youth as Saul wanted him dead. He was forced to leave the comfort and security of his home and flee for his life. He wandered through deserts, wilderness, mountains, hills, valleys, and caves. He had to take shelter in these inhospitable and unsafe places.

But many of the Psalms written by David during these times show us that David's trust was in the Lord Almighty. He knew that

God was in charge of everything, including his own life, "In God I trust and am not afraid. What can man do to me?" (Psalm 56:11). So he committed his ways to God, and it is this act of surrendering to God that became his source of safety and security,

> Have mercy on me, my God, have mercy on me,
> > for in you I take refuge.
> I will take refuge in the shadow of your wings
> > until the disaster has passed.
>
> > > (Psalm 57:1)

God protected and preserved David's life even when he was without a home.

David's writings in the Psalms demonstrate his unwavering confidence in God. When things got worse, he lamented over his plight but ultimately turned to God in worship and submission. In the midst of pain, he found comfort and strength in God's presence. His heart overflowed so much with love for God that it spilled over to his writings. Whether he was wandering in the wilderness or sitting on the throne as king of Israel, David recognized that it was his relationship with God that was his treasure and crown. His intimacy with God was his protection and provision. He felt safe and satisfied in the presence of God.

We, too, can find the deepest satisfaction and pleasure when we spend time in God's presence. To dwell with God is our greatest blessing.

God's Dwelling Place

In the Old Testament, the tabernacle was considered God's dwelling place. The presence of the Holy God made it holy. Access to the tabernacle was restricted to priests. Ordinary people were considered too unclean to enter into God's holy presence at their own will.

But Jesus turned this concept of God's dwelling place on its head.

The New Testament clarifies that the bodies of those redeemed by Jesus are the temples of the Holy Spirit, "Do you not know that your bodies are temples of the Holy Spirit, who is in you, whom you have received from God? You are not your own." (1 Corinthians 6:19). We become not just the house of God but the temple of God, Christ being our builder. Christ imputes His righteousness to us and makes us so clean that the Holy Spirit inhabits us. The need for human priests to intercede for us or for animal sacrifices to make atonement for our sins has been done away with because of Jesus's death on the cross.

The Bible takes it a step further, calling God's redeemed people a "royal priesthood" (1 Peter 2:9). While our physical bodies are spiritual houses of God, our spiritual status is that of priests, laying our lives down in the service of God, representing our Lord and Master to the world, participating in worship, and constantly being drawn closer to Him. It's a beautiful picture of how united believers are with the Trinity, both physically and spiritually (John 4:23).

The more we love and serve God, the stronger the bond gets. Our home with God is essentially a metaphor for this unity of spirit between man and God. It is a home that is being continually built up, restored, strengthened, reinforced, and expanded.

We were created to be a house of God, a temple of God. We were made to have an intimate relationship with Him. We were shaped to crave eternal unity with God.

My Home

It took me years on the road to realize I felt completely at home when I was in God's presence.

When we love God and set our heart on pleasing Him, we invite Him to take charge of all areas of our lives. His presence inhabits our entire being. We cannot compartmentalize our faith and restrict it to Sunday mornings or to certain aspects of our lives. We are called to surrender our whole lives to Jesus out of love for and devotion to Him, "Therefore, I urge you, brothers and sisters, in view of God's mercy, to offer your bodies as a living sacrifice, holy and pleasing to God—this is your true and proper worship" (Romans 12:1).

In the midst of unfamiliar surroundings or unprepared transitions we can feel overwhelmed, alone, or abandoned. But when we make our home with God, His presence will see us through in a supernatural way, strengthening and refining our faith as we press on.

The benefit of making our home with God is that external circumstances cannot wreak havoc with our souls. No matter what happens, we can know that we are loved and valued by a God who knows everything about us, who watches over us all the time, who longs to help us, who is eager to bless us, and who has good plans for us.

Our home with God is steadfast and permanent, just as He Himself is immutable and eternal. Our earthly home can only be an imperfect and incomplete model of heaven, that points to our homelessness on earth. Only when we join Jesus in heaven will we find our forever, perfect home.

Reach In

1. What does homelessness mean to you?

2. Where or when do you most feel at home?

3. What is your definition of home? How is God included in your definition of home?

4. What is preventing you from surrendering all areas of your life to God?

5. Do you long for more intimacy with God? How will you take your needs to God in prayer today?

Reach Out

Think of ways you can help the homeless in your city or town. Do you know someone who's struggling in their faith? Invite them to study the Bible with you on a regular basis. Let them know you're praying for them.

Reach Up

Dear Father in Heaven,

Your love is my life. Thank You for loving me and being with me through all the ups and downs of life. The world around me has changed and is changing. But You have remained the same. You have never left my side. Your grace has been sufficient. You have kept all Your promises to me. I love You. I long for more of You. I commit my future into Your hands. I know that no matter what happens, I will have a home in You. In You alone I place my trust. In You, I find shelter, comfort, peace, joy, hope, and strength. I look forward to going with You to the place You have prepared for me. Thank You for the assurance of a permanent home in eternity. To You be all glory and honor and praise!

Amen.

CHAPTER 8
Homesick for Heaven

*Therefore we are always confident and know that as long
as we are at home in the body we are away from the Lord.*

2 Corinthians 5:6

I heard the pitter-patter of rain while I was still in bed one morning. Rain in September was unusual in California. I went about my morning chores, and the incessant rain provided the perfect backdrop for nostalgia to brew and memories to unfold.

I sat on the porch and sipped my morning cup of tea; the smell of drenched leaves and wet dirt and the sight of leftover rain drops on my window triggered a dull ache in my heart. Waves of memories of the Indian monsoon season of June to September flooded my mind, drowning me in sadness. An unbearable yearning for my former home made my stomach churn.

I lived almost thirty years of my life in India where the rainy season lasts for four months in a year—June to September. And when it rains, it pours and roars, washing clean the dirty roads and dusty trees. Most people don't know that India is home to two of the wettest places on earth. Cherrapunji and Mawsynrum, two towns in northeast India, receive an average of about 452 inches of rain annually.

Summer precedes the monsoon season, lasting from March to May. And Indian summers are so brutal that people of the subcontinent look forward to rain like children who eagerly await their birthdays. All summer long, our parched souls and sweaty bodies long to be drenched in rain.

Throughout June, we watch the skies in anticipation. Through the noise of street vendors haggling, cars honking, loud aunties gossiping, TV news anchors debating, and Bollywood music blaring, we listen for the lazy rumble of thunder. We wait for the comatose clouds to wake up from their slumber. We watch for birds in the sky disappearing to their secret hiding spots.

When I was a little girl, my sister and I used to run to the roof to catch the first droplets of the first rain of the year as our mom rushed to the balcony to release the clean, dried clothes from the clothesline. We opened our mouths to drink from the clouds. We danced and laughed.

The nightmare of summer was over.

As one season replaced another, our routines and menus changed. Hot cups of chai replaced coconut water and lemonade. *Samosas* and *pakoras* replaced mangoes and ice cream. Rain dictated how we went about our day, what kind of family fun we had, and what music we enjoyed. In popular Bollywood movies, rain sets the perfect scene for romance to bud and blossom. One can create a playlist of Bollywood songs celebrating romance in the rain.

But the rainy season was not all rosy and romantic. It did cause some inconvenience but we learned to cope with it. Flooded streets forged new routes and roundabout commutes while the sound of rain became white noise that lulled us to sleep. Wet shoes, slow-moving traffic, and power outages became part and parcel of everyday life. Compared to the sweltering heat that sapped us of our energy, rain breathed new life into us and energized our senses.

The twenty-nine monsoon seasons that I spent in India are etched in the deepest places of my mind and heart. No wonder rain makes me homesick.

But it's not just rain.

Walking into an Indian grocery, watching a Bollywood movie, or hearing two people talk in my native tongue, Telugu, triggers homesickness. I also miss my family and friends, especially when I'm going through a difficult time or celebrating good times like birthdays and anniversaries.

I did not realize how strong my ties to my homeland were until I became an immigrant. I was not forced to leave home. The choice to leave home was mine. But that doesn't mean putting down roots in another country is easy or effortless. Mobility and displacement add a new dimension to homesickness, making it particularly taxing for immigrants.

Immigrants are often seen as resilient and admired for their work ethic and drive to succeed. What many people do not realize is that many of us pay a hefty emotional price for our success. Whether we are conscious of it or not, an underlying sense of loss and a persistent homesickness never leave us.

The Anatomy of Homesickness

We have all experienced homesickness at some point in our lives, in different ways and at varying levels. Certain sights, smells, and sounds can trigger feelings that make us long for a place or a home we've left behind. We can miss moments in our lives when we had felt accepted and loved, secure and safe.

Glancing at family photos, recreating a meal that we used to enjoy with our families when we were young, listening to an old song on the radio, or running into a friend from our school days can make us relive times from our past. These thoughts, especially the good ones, soothe our soul and make us yearn for home. We can feel real pain—emotional and sometimes even physical. There is no medication available to help ease the symptoms.

Home is the only cure.

The truth is that the connection between home and soul is not a mystery since the longing for home is built into our DNA. When God made man and woman, He placed them in a home He created for them, the garden of Eden. When Adam and Eve disobeyed God, sin corrupted them and altered their relationship with God. Banished from the garden, they were separated from God.

The fall was mankind's moment of displacement. It made us spiritual refugees. Uprooted and exiled, we find ourselves shut out of the perfect home. What made the garden of Eden Adam's perfect home was not the perfection and beauty of the place itself, nor the delectable fruit and myriad creatures that filled it, nor the love he had for Eve. The garden of Eden was the perfect home because God dwelt there, walking and talking with Adam and Eve. The first couple lacked nothing because they enjoyed God's friendship. Intimacy with God met all their needs for love, security, stability, shelter, sustenance, and safety.

As fallen people who live in a broken world, we fear being displaced and abandoned from our earthly homes. We spend our time and energy on earth searching for a place we can call home, trying to build a home that will not fall apart or be taken away. Even when we think we have finally settled into a home, restlessness and discontentment can lurk under the surface of our emotions. For some of us, no fancy condo, spacious single-family home, or beach house can truly feel at home.

Homelessness was a direct consequence of the first couple's rebellion. The same homelessness can plague us. This cohabitation of homelessness with a desire for a permanent home creates in us a discomfort that is hard to explain or escape. While most people cannot put a finger on it and spend their entire lives in search of answers to the riddle, Christians have the privilege of knowing what this tension represents—heavenly homesickness.

Homesick for Heaven

God's adopted children are coheirs with Christ and members of His kingdom. We subscribe to the rules of God's kingdom which are in direct opposition to worldly values. Citizens of heaven are misfits on earth. Our discontentment with our earthly home is a natural outcome of our heavenly citizenship. Our restlessness stems from our close relationship with God and our longing to be united with Him eternally in heaven.

We are homeless on earth and homesick for heaven.

Having lived in at least ten different homes in the first thirteen years of marriage, I'm no stranger to homesickness. But it took me a while to realize what it means to feel homesick for heaven.

Earthly homesickness looks to the past and wants to relive it. Heavenly homesickness, on the other hand, looks to the future. It is not based on past memories but on future hope. It's the reason why the analogy of a bride waiting for her groom aptly explains how we, the church, look forward to being united with Christ.

A bride waits joyfully to wed her groom and to build a new home with him. She hopes to spend the rest of her life in bliss with her beloved. Being homesick for heaven means just like a bride, we too, long to be one with the Lover of our souls. Unlike an earthly bride, our hope is not in a husband who is human—weak, flawed, and unstable. Our Bridegroom is Jesus Christ, the King of kings, the Author and Sustainer of life, the epitome of faithfulness, and the essence of holiness. We look forward to the consummation of our salvation with our Lord and Savior. We look forward to a lifetime of togetherness with Him in the New Jerusalem.

Let's take a closer look at what our future in heaven looks like.

A Restored Earth and Resurrected Body

When Jesus returns, the earth as we know it will be destroyed, "But the day of the Lord will come like a thief. The heavens will disappear with a roar; the elements will be destroyed by fire, and the earth and everything done in it will be laid bare" (2 Peter 3:10). After this cataclysmic event, the Holy City of Jerusalem will come down from heaven to form "a new heaven and a new earth" (Revelation 21:1–2). United with heaven, the earth will be renewed and restored to its original state before sin tarnished it. This unadulterated new heaven and new earth will be our abode.

Similar to the earth's rebirth, our bodies will also undergo a transformation. Our earthly bodies are prone to disease and decay. The aches and pains of growing older are proof that are bodies are giving way, nearing their end. Our mortal bodies bear the brunt of a fallen world. Stress and sickness ravage our bodies, which can fall victim to pandemics and epidemics.

If we believe in Jesus's resurrection, we must believe that we, too, will be resurrected (1 Corinthians 15:22–23). After Jesus's resurrection, he met with His disciples and ate with them. When Thomas doubted who He was, Jesus asked Thomas to touch the nail marks on his hands and feel his side (John 20:27). The remarkable thing about this incident was that Jesus entered through locked doors. Will our heavenly bodies be like Jesus's resurrected body? We will know the answer only when we get to heaven.

The apostle Paul uses the analogy of a seed to explain how our mortal bodies will be raised up into heavenly bodies, "The body that is sown is perishable, it is raised imperishable; it is sown in dishonor, it is raised in glory; it is sown in weakness, it is raised in power; it is sown a natural body, it is raised a spiritual body" (1 Corinthians 15:42–44). When does this resurrection take place? The Bible suggests that when we die, our soul is united with God. But our bodies will be raised up when Jesus returns to earth.

This truth lights me up. No matter how healthy I eat or how much I exercise my body and brain, I know that one day my body will fade away. But a new day will come when I gain a glorious body that will far surpass the capabilities and limitations of my former body. I will not have to worry about keeping my body in perfect health and shape.

The resurrected body of the believer will be far superior to the earthly body. We can look forward to the day when our minds, bodies, and souls will be made anew, perfectly Christ-like. Our hearts will overflow with wholesome love for God and one another. Our minds will be perfectly aligned with God's.

We can also draw great comfort from knowing that those who have passed away are not just resting in peace but rejoicing in glory with Jesus. A happy reunion awaits in the new heaven and new earth.

Satan's Fall

When we think of heaven, we can envision a place where the devil has no power and no authority. He will be completely and forever destroyed, "And the devil, who deceived them, was thrown into the lake of burning sulfur, where the beast and the false prophet had been thrown. They will be tormented day and night for ever and ever" (Revelation 20:10).

Because of the absence of sin, we will be free from all temptation and guilt. There will be no more broken relationships. Holiness will saturate heaven's citizens. Injustice, unfairness, hatred, and conflicts will vanish. We will not experience jealousy or envy, only love. We will not know fear. We will also not have to strive to trust and obey God. Our faith in God will be pure and refined, without any impurities.

When I think of Satan's impending and inevitable doom, I'm relieved and hopeful. The wickedness and depravity I witness can sometimes infuriate and frustrate me. News of rising human trafficking, child abuse, domestic violence, financial scams, racial oppression, homicides, and genocides can make me sad and depressed. I can do whatever I can to help, but nothing seems to stem the growth of violence and greed and injustice. However, I know that my Redeemer, the Alpha and the Omega, will one day put an end to all evil, and I cannot wait to see Satan defeated.

The knowledge of Satan's end also causes me to see him as a temporary and weak foe. I do not need to fear him. Jesus has already defeated him on the cross and will obliterate him forever when He returns.

God's Dwelling Place

The apostle John envisions the New Jerusalem as a city embellished with precious metals and jewels. But its most attractive and fundamental aspect is that it is God's dwelling place: "And I heard a loud voice from the throne saying, 'Look! God's dwelling place is now among the people, and he will dwell with them. They will be his people, and God himself will be with them and be their God'" (Revelation 21:3).

God's blueprint for mankind finds its culmination in the New Jerusalem (Leviticus 26:11–12). This was His intention all along, when He created the garden of Eden, when He instituted the tabernacle with Moses, when He commissioned the temple in Jerusalem, and when He sent His own Son, in the flesh, to dwell among us (John 1:14).

In heaven, we will spend all our time with God, worshipping Him with our new bodies. There will be no separation between God and us. Perfect union and intimacy with God are guaranteed. Like a gentle, caring Father, "'He will wipe every tear from [our] eyes. There will be no more death' or mourning or crying or pain, for the old order of things has passed away" (Revelation 21:4).

The book of Revelation explains that because God dwells in the heavenly city, there will be no need for a temple. There will also be no need for the brilliance of the sun or the moon since the Holy City will shine with the glory of God.

My heart races whenever I close my eyes and ponder my heavenly residence. How wonderful it will be to talk and walk with God and see Him face-to-face (1 John 3:2)! Here on earth, I have been communicating with God in my mind without seeing His face or body. It will be breathtaking to finally behold the tangible presence of my Father, to hear Him call my name, and to run into His arms.

As if living with God is not amazing enough, we will also reign with Christ,

> If we died with him,
>> we will also live with him;
> if we endure,
>> we will also reign with him.
>> (2 Timothy 2:11–12)

As coheirs with Christ, we have the privilege of ruling with Him and sharing in His glory.

Judgment and Rewards

When some believers think of heaven, they may feel fearful instead of hopeful. A common myth that incites dread is that we will be judged for our sins. But the Bible assures us that we will not face punishment. Jesus stood in our place and bore the punishment for our sins. Once and for all. God's grace has absolved us of the consequences of sin.

We will appear before God's judgment seat, but we will not be condemned (Romans 8:1). As those covered by the blood of the Lamb, the citizens of God's kingdom will receive pardon and rewards. Our names are written in the Lamb's Book of Life, confirming eternal life as our inheritance.

Those who know the truth and reject it will be judged for their sins. In Luke 16, Jesus narrates the parable of a rich man and a beggar named Lazarus who lay at the gate of the rich man's mansion. The rich man lived a luxurious life, while Lazarus was so poor and wretched that the dogs licked at his sores as he waited for scraps from the rich man's table.

The status and condition of the two men were reversed when they died. While Lazarus was carried away by angels to Abraham's side, the rich man faced torment in Hades. Through this parable Jesus clarifies that while believers will rejoice in God's presence with God's people, unbelievers will suffer eternal separation from God.

This is a hard truth to digest, but we must remember that "God is a righteous judge" (Psalm 7:11). He is merciful and gives people several chances to repent and turn from their ways. He will judge people on how they respond when they encounter the truth of God's saving grace. God's justice and mercy do not contradict each other. Rather, they perfectly unite and align with His character.

The day of Jesus's return will be a day of judgment.

The punishment for those who do not give their lives to Jesus will be brutal and eternal (Matthew 24:38–39). But those who have surrendered their lives to Jesus will be rewarded according to their good deeds: "For the Son of Man is going to come in his Father's glory with his angels, and then he will reward each person according to what they have done" (Matthew 16:27).

Jesus will come to judge the world and to reward those who follow Him. This heavenly truth can heighten our anticipation for the Lord. Justice will be served. Righteousness will prevail. Rewards will be presented.

The greatest dividend, better than the treasures or crowns, is fellowship with Jesus. Our love for God fuels our pining to be ultimately united with Him.

Longing for Heaven

This desire to be united with our Lord only increases as we draw closer to Him and want more of Him. Our dissatisfaction with our earthly home and our homesickness for our heavenly residence is a good thing. It is God-given and God-approved. It is a gift that is especially granted to those who love God and find fulfillment and joy in His divine presence and person.

Paul alludes to homesickness in his letter to the Corinthians, "For we know that if the earthly tent we live in is destroyed, we have a building from God, an eternal house in heaven, not built by human hands. Meanwhile we groan, longing to be clothed instead with our heavenly dwelling" (2 Corinthians 5:1–2). Peter, too, refers to our bodies merely as earthly tents—frail and fragile (2 Peter 1:13). Tents do not imply security or stability. They wear and tear and tatter easily and eventually wear out. The earthiness of our bodies points to the transitory and fragile nature of our existence and amplifies our dissatisfaction with temporal pleasures.

While outwardly we age and decay, inwardly we are being renewed and becoming more like Christ. Burdened by suffering and trials and our own weaknesses, we cry out for the time when our bodies will be resurrected (2 Corinthians 5:4). Our heavenly bodies are marvelous buildings, not tents. Our eternal house is not built by human hands. It's as if we're naked pilgrims on earth, craving to be clothed with our heavenly dwelling. Only in heaven will we possess our resurrected bodies and attain perfect Christlikeness.

This pining for our heavenly abode is ingrained in us since we were made for Christlikeness (2 Corinthians 5:5). The Holy Spirit living within us serves as guarantee for our future with God. He helps us persevere through the rocky paths of life. He cheers us on, reminding us of God's promises and plans. He encourages us to fix our eyes on our fantastic destination. The Holy Spirit is responsible for our heightened feelings of homesickness. He writes God's words on our hearts, motivating us to live in obedience to God. He makes us long for intimacy and oneness with God.

David captures this hunger for God beautifully in many of his writings but this passage (Psalm 84:1–4) stands out to me:

> How lovely is your dwelling place,
>   LORD Almighty!

My soul yearns, even faints,
　　for the courts of the LORD;
my heart and my flesh cry out
　　for the living God.
Even the sparrow has found a home,
　　and the swallow a nest for herself,
　　where she may have her young—
a place near your altar,
　　LORD Almighty, my King and my God.
Blessed are those who dwell in your house;
　　they are ever praising you.

Looking forward to heaven as our eternal dwelling place with God means living daily with the knowledge that the earth is not our home.

When we embrace our identity as foreigners on earth and citizens of heaven, our craving for our home in heaven intensifies,

All these people were still living by faith when they died. They did not receive the things promised; they only saw them and welcomed them from a distance, admitting that they were foreigners and strangers on earth. People who say such things show that they are looking for a country of their own. If they had been thinking of the country they had left, they would have had opportunity to return. Instead, they were longing for a better country—a heavenly one. (Hebrews 11:13–16)

Migration and constant change have rewired my concept of home. Home remains elusive, distant, and ambiguous, and homesickness has become a faithful friend. When I visit India, I feel homesick for America. As I grow closer to God, my struggles and confusion become superficialities and give way to a different kind of homesickness.

I do not have memories of heaven, like I do of my former homeland. But from time to time, I experience heaven right here on earth.

Whenever I see God's hand at work in my life, I catch a glimpse of heaven.

Whenever I meditate on His Word and receive precious treasures of insight or revelation about His character, I touch heaven.

Whenever I experience His supernatural comfort through a time of intense suffering, I taste a slice of heaven.

Whenever I worship God together with people of different ethnicities and cultures, I am surrounded by the harmonies of heaven.

These encounters make me want more of God and yearn for my true heavenly home. I know what it is like to be a foreigner and to feel out of place. Seeing myself as a spiritual immigrant whose citizenship is in heaven makes me crave for a permanent home with God and His people. This holy homesickness will find its cure when I'm united with my Savior in heaven.

Reach In

1. How does the knowledge of eternal blessings in heaven draw you closer to God?

   _____

2. Do you desire more intimacy with God? If you don't, how will you pray about it today?

   _____

3. Are you homesick for heaven? Why, or why not?

   _____

4. Which particular feature of the new heaven and new earth appeals to you the most? Why?

   _____

5. What can you do now to prepare yourself to see Jesus face-to-face?

   _____

Reach Out

Make a list of your unbelieving friends and family members. Commit to praying for their salvation on a regular basis. Ask God to give you an opportunity to share the gospel and the truths about heaven with them.

Reach Up

Dear Father in Heaven,

I worship and adore You. You are righteous, compassionate, forgiving, good, and sovereign. I delight in Your presence, and I want more of You. I am grateful that You have allotted me an eternal inheritance. I am humbled that my name is written in the Lamb's Book of Life. I am in awe of Your mercy and grace. I am amazed at Your plans for the redemption of the earth and its people. Thank You for the assurance that my body will be renewed. I believe that in heaven there will be no more sin, sickness, suffering, or death. You will dwell with me and all my brothers and sisters forever. I will be able to look into Your eyes and see You smiling back at me. How precious are the thoughts of my future! My heart aches for heaven. Come, Lord Jesus, and take me home.

Amen.

CHAPTER 9
Homeward Bound

Therefore keep watch, because you do not know on what day your Lord will come.

Matthew 24:42

"What do you look forward to the most when you visit India?" a podcast host asked when she interviewed me about my immigrant experience.

"I look forward to spending time with my family. Most of my immediate and extended family live in India. And I eat as much Indian food as I can."

After a brief pause, I went on. "The minute I land at the Hyderabad International Airport and set foot on Indian soil, I breathe a sigh of relief."

It's true. When I get out of the plane, my body experiences a range of emotions. Excitement, relief, tiredness. The moment I land in India is a culmination of months of planning and waiting and dreaming.

My family tries to visit India every other year so that we don't spend all our summers abroad. Preparation for our visits is exciting, and usually involves a lot of planning. Flights are booked about six months in advance, which is when I start packing my bags. Shopping for our Indian family and friends is a huge part of our preparation. I always buy a crisp white shirt for my dad, handbags for my mom, clothes and makeup for my sister, and toys for my niece. My husband also shops for his parents, sister, three brothers, and six nieces and nephews. Stuff cannot make up for our absence, but we want our families to feel loved even if we were not always present to comfort them during difficult times and celebrate good times with them.

A surge of excitement marks the days and weeks leading up to my departure from America. I alternate between superwoman-like productive days and several lazy hours daydreaming about my trip to India. My mind gets cramped with mental lists—lists of places I want to visit, people I want to spend time with, things I want to buy, and food I want to eat.

The Ride Home

The journey to India from America is long and takes about twenty hours by flight with one or two layovers. Traveling internationally, especially in the economy class, is uncomfortable and burdensome because I can't sleep in a seated position. Sleep deprivation makes me cranky, turning me into a different person. My neck hurts, my legs feel heavy from lack of movement, and my mind is numb from watching one movie after another.

After spending hours with passengers who are probably equally uncomfortable in their seats, I go from flashing smiles and being chatty to frowning, rolling my eyes, and shooting angry glances at mothers with crying toddlers. My bucket of patience empties drop by drop till I become frustrated, waiting to be back on earth, instead of journeying through endless clouds.

But I know, with every passing hour, I'm getting closer to home. The anticipation and excitement make the difficult flight bearable.

When the plane lands, I feel like a bird, free to go wherever I please, freed from the cage of an airplane that ironically looks much like a bird itself. The sleepy passengers on the flight all wake up at once, eager to deplane. A frenzy of activity follows. Cell phones buzz. Passengers squeeze through the narrow aisle, trying to get ahead of others. There is just one more hurdle left. The ordeal of entering the airport of a foreign country.

By the time we pass through customs and immigration and collect our bags at the Hyderabad International airport, my family is hungry and tired. We yawn and stretch, glad to be standing on solid ground. Looking haggard and a bit disoriented, like animals who emerge out of winter hibernation, we smell funny. Unkempt hair, sleepy eyes, sweaty bodies, wrinkled clothes. *When was the last time we brushed our teeth?* We don't care.

We have reached India. We are in Hyderabad.

So we push through the fatigue and the irritation, our hearts dizzy with expectation. We're almost home.

The long taxi ride home from the airport in the wee hours of the morning gives us a peek into the paradox that is India. We pass by tall office buildings and fancy gated communities as well as homeless people sleeping on the streets. The taxi driver cares little for traffic rules. He talks with a relative loudly on the cell phone while he honks and swerves, changing lanes carelessly. My initial reaction is shock. But I know I'll get so used to Indian traffic that in a week I'll stop stressing about it.

My body screams for a nap, but my emotions are so overloaded that I find it impossible to rest in the hour-long taxi ride to our home. My son pulls my sleeve and asks me for the hundredth time, "Are we there yet?" I shoot my don't-mess-with-me look at him. Ryan wriggles and squirms. By now, Simon, Ryan, and I have reached our thresholds for patience. Silenced by grumpiness and tiredness, we can barely wait for the taxi to reach my parents' apartment—our oasis, our refuge.

When we arrive at my parents' door, relief gushes through our bodies. Our parents welcome us in their night clothes. My mom squeals with delight when she embraces Ryan. My father opens his arms to receive us. I notice more wrinkles and lines on my parents' faces. I look around my family home. The decades-old furniture, the white-orange curtains, the pictures on the walls, the position of the television—nothing has changed over the years.

I want to give the home a hug. I want to give familiarity a big squeeze. I feel a sense of comfort, joy, and loss wash over me as I allow my body to plop onto the couch in the living room. It is the best couch in the world. I know I'm home.

Going Home

We will be home one day.

Our journey on earth might be long or short, easy or weary. But we have the assurance that the hills and the valleys, the meadows and the wilderness, and the straight and narrow paths ultimately lead us to the promised destination. The Bible urges us to get ready for our future home that awaits us at the end of our earthly pilgrimage.

Jesus taught that citizens of the kingdom of God must live with eternity in mind. The way we live out our lives here on earth demonstrates our readiness for heaven. Every decision, every action counts. We do not know when our lives will end or when Jesus will come back. God sets the expiration date for our journey and keeps it hidden from us. He expects us, however, to be prepared.

I learned the value of readiness when I was thirty-four weeks pregnant. My husband and I had packed our go bags for the hospital knowing I could go into labor anytime. We had taken Lamaze classes to learn how to manage labor pain. Newborn clothes were washed and neatly folded in a new closet, and diapers of different sizes were stacked. We turned down invites to events and gatherings and dialed down long-term plans. We lived one hour and one day at a time, our hearts primed with almost uncontainable happiness and excitement, waiting to see, smell, and touch our baby.

Like expectant parents, like immigrants who return home, God's children can look forward to their certain future with joyful anticipation. But the promise of eternal security is not a pass for lazy living or complacent faith.

Be Ready

Using three parables in Matthew 24 and 25—the parable of the faithful and wise servant, the parable of the ten virgins, and the parable of the bags of money—Jesus demonstrates how we can be alert and ready. Our conduct in this life has eternal implications.

In the parable of the bags of money, a master entrusts each of his servants with a specific amount before he leaves on a journey. The first servant multiplies his five bags of money to ten. The second servant, too, invests his two bags and doubles what he had been entrusted with. The third servant does not invest but takes the one bag of money he was given and buries it to keep it safe.

When the master returns, He lavishes praise on the first two servants, calling them good and faithful. He appreciates them for their stewardship and gives them more of his wealth. The third servant receives a strong rebuke from the master for not putting his money to good use. The money is taken away from him.

Jesus expects His followers to use the talents and time entrusted to them to further His kingdom on earth. Each of us accomplishes this purpose in different ways since we are gifted differently, according to our abilities and God's grace. Our omniscient God places us in specific situations and gives us particular opportunities so that we can maximize our gifts to impact the world in powerful ways.

Over the past decade, I have visited India at least five times. The days leading up to my departure from America are consumed with a single-minded focus on planning and preparation for my trip to India. The thought that I will be going home lingers at the back of my mind, whether I'm washing dishes or hanging out with friends.

I want to remember, however, even when I'm not traveling overseas, that I'm homeward bound. I want my life to be abuzz with the excitement of going to heaven. I do not want to be lazy or afraid like the servant in Jesus's parable who hid his bag of money. I want to multiply my talents in God's service so I can hear God whisper in my ear, "Well done, good and faithful servant."

One of the important characteristics of citizens of heaven is faithful stewardship of gifts. We are called to invest in sharpening and growing our God-given abilities, proactively seeking out opportunities to use our talents.

God blesses us when we dedicate our lives to magnifying His name on earth. Our selfless and diligent management of skills and resources pleases Him. He sees how we labor in our prayer closets, interceding for our church and country. He takes notice when we persevere in training our children in godliness. God knows how relentlessly we pursue reconciliation and peace. He watches us fight for justice and speak up for the voiceless. And He rewards our faithfulness by granting us more opportunities to serve Him and by expanding our circles of influence. The blessings continue to eternity. "For the Son of Man is going to come in his Father's glory with his angels, and then he will reward each person according to what they have done" (Matthew 16:27).

Treasures in Heaven

We do not know what heavenly rewards look like, but they will be better than the best of earthly trophies and medals. Brilliant and glorious, they will be more satisfying than any reward we would have received in our lifetime. Paul explains how we can store up eternal wealth in practical ways.

> Command those who are rich in this present world not to be arrogant nor to put their hope in wealth, which is so uncertain, but to put their hope in God, who richly provides us with everything for our enjoyment. Command them to do good, to be rich in good deeds, and to be generous and willing to share. In this way they will lay up treasure for themselves as a firm foundation for the coming age, so that they may take hold of the life that is truly life. (1 Timothy 6:17–19)

Our immigrant identity reminds us to set our sights on our home in heaven and to direct our attention and energy toward those things that impact God's kingdom, both now and in the future. Knowing that we are homeward bound energizes us to make it our life's goal to prepare for eternity. The excitement of gazing upon the face of our Lord Jesus and enjoying His presence for eternity drives us to finish our pilgrim journey strong. We leave no stone unturned in service to our King. We do not hesitate to sacrifice our desires or pleasures to ensure that God's kingdom on earth advances.

Moses gave up the luxury of royalty and the potential future of becoming the leader of Egypt for the sake of greater rewards, "By faith Moses, when he had grown up, refused to be known as the son of Pharaoh's daughter. He chose to be mistreated along with the people of God rather than to enjoy the fleeting pleasures of sin. He regarded disgrace for the sake of Christ as of greater value than the treasures of Egypt, because he was looking ahead to his reward" (Hebrews 11:24–26).

Moses inspires me to examine my priorities and live a life that reflects a forward-thinking vision.

My initial years in America as an immigrant were marked with loneliness and fruitlessness. I took my eyes off my identity as a citizen of heaven and focused on becoming a well-settled and well-adjusted earthly immigrant, forgetting to look ahead to my eternal inheritance. But God was committed to drawing me to His side and maturing my faith.

Immersing myself in Scripture illuminated my mind so I could see my pilgrim journey through the lens of eternity. He revealed to me that I could find rootedness, belonging, and significance in God alone. God intentionally orchestrated the events in my life so that I could take hold of the purpose He had for me and pursue it with passion and courage. God wanted me on His team, working for His kingdom, so I could be prepared for Christ's return.

My citizenship and influence in heaven renders each and every earthly thought, word, and deed eternally significant. Every trial I go through, every blessing I receive from God, every relationship I form has a profound impact on both my life on earth as well as my residence in heaven.

Holy Living

Another important aspect of our preparation is commitment to holy living. The apostle Peter presents our glorious future and the inevitable end of the world as an incentive and driver for the pursuit of holiness.

> Since everything will be destroyed in this way, what kind of people ought you to be? You ought to live holy and godly lives as you look forward to the day of God and speed its coming. That day will bring about the destruction of the heavens by fire, and the elements will melt in the heat. But in keeping with his promise we are looking forward to a new heaven and a new earth, where righteousness dwells. So then, dear friends, since you are looking forward to this, make every effort to be found spotless, blameless and at peace with him. (2 Peter 3:11–14)

As we grow in intimacy with God, we develop a right attitude toward sin, perceiving it as harmful, contagious, and the root of all evil. We hate sin because God hates sin. The practice of daily repentance is crucial not only in rooting out sin from our lives but also in appreciating God's grace and humbling ourselves before Him. The more we yield to the Holy Spirit, who convicts us of sin, the less we give in to the desires of the flesh.

We will, no doubt, fail sometimes and give in to temptation. But God is faithful to forgive us, and the Holy Spirit assures us of our righteousness in Christ. When we fall, He helps us get back up and continue on our journey. He strengthens our commitment to follow Jesus.

Here on earth, we will never be able to fully lead a sinless life, but the Holy Spirit empowers us to overcome sinful thoughts and habits and grow in holiness. When our struggles with temptations and sins weaken us, He enables us to contend for our faith and rest in the knowledge of God's limitless supply of grace. He increases our desire to love and obey God. Holy living has more to do with the heart than just moral behavior. The Holy Spirit transforms our mind and heart, so we eagerly desire to become more like Jesus.

Our holiness testifies to the holiness of God. People can see how we cling to biblical values without compromise. Our testimony brings honor and glory to God, identifying us as people who bear His name.

As foreigners on earth looking ahead to the Lord's coming, we must "clothe [ourselves] with the Lord Jesus Christ" and not occupy ourselves with gratifying our carnal desires (Romans 13:14). And we can look forward to a future when we will be free from the clutches of our sinful nature, living and breathing holiness.

Forward-Minded

Crises, sickness, trials, and sin can make our pilgrim journey arduous and burdensome. Sometimes, more than suffering, it's the prolonged periods of going through the motions of life without keeping eternity in mind that deprives us of joy and purpose. Without direction or a clear path, we become wanderers in exile.

Our journey as immigrants on earth, however, can be replete with adventures and blessings. God created us with a purpose and bestowed us with talents we can utilize to participate in His grand plan that stretches from the earth to heaven. As God's children, His holy priests, and His servants, we are at the center of His blueprint for mankind. When we are consumed with fulfilling His plans and reflecting His holiness, we can experience unspeakable joy even in the midst of suffering. The anticipation of our rewards and glory in our future home helps us stay on course and makes us see our struggles in the light of eternity.

The people of Israel wandered in the desert for forty years before being able to enter the promised land. They learned to follow the pillar of cloud by day and the pillar of fire by night (Exodus 13:21–22). They pitched their tents when the pillar of cloud or fire came to a rest. And they picked up and moved when the cloud lifted. They did not know what came next on the road, but they knew their destination. They did not know *when*, so they lived in readiness for *whenever*, holding on to the promises of God. On the move, they were being taught the meaning of the wear and tear of the temporal present versus the promise of a lasting future in Canaan.

Paul reminds us that "this world in its present form is passing away" (1 Corinthians 7:31), and that "outwardly we [too] are wasting away" (2 Corinthians 4:16). Our relationship with God and our future with Him, however, are certain and long-lasting. So then let us not get caught up in worldly affairs, and let us not give our physical bodies and earthly homes undue importance. We can ask God to "teach us to number our days" (Psalm 90:12) so we can live wisely between mortality and immortality with the blessed hope of heaven bubbling over from our hearts.

Our immigrant identity reminds us that we are simply passing through and that each step on this journey is taking us closer to our eternal home. Our God-given heavenly citizenship informs us of the connectedness between our testimony on earth and our glory in heaven. What a privilege it is to know that our actions on earth can be worthy of treasures in heaven! What a joy in knowing that mere humans like us can participate in God's plans on earth and make our home with Him in the heavenly realms!

Reach In

1. Are you excited about spending eternity with Jesus in the new heaven and new earth?

---

2. Do you feel you're ready for Jesus's return? What does readiness mean to you?

---

3. How are you investing in heavenly treasures?

---

4. What thought patterns or attitudes are keeping you from leading a holy life?

---

5. How does the promise of a glorious future with God influence your current lifestyle?

Reach Out

Write a note of gratitude or encouragement to your pastors or ministry leaders. Remind them that their labor is not in vain and that eternal rewards await them in heaven. Let them also know how they have positively impacted your faith.

Reach Up

Dear Father in Heaven,

Thank you for the gift of eternal life. Thank you for the promise of heaven. I look forward to the day when I can live with You forever. In heaven, there will be no more tears or toiling. I will be free to serve You with all my heart and strength. I can't wait to be home with You. Remind me that I'm on my way home, that my life on earth is a journey with a set destination. I want to be alert and ready. I seek Your guidance and wisdom to live a holy life.

Anoint me with your Holy Spirit and fill me with excitement for both the work on earth as well as the rewards in heaven. Help me identify my talents and seek out ways to use them for Your plans and purposes. Keep me from getting entangled in worldly things. Direct my attention to heaven and focus my thoughts and intentions on Your will for my life.

Amen.

Section Three
Community

CHAPTER 10
Craving for Community

*Therefore, as we have opportunity, let us do good to all
people, especially to those who belong to the family of
believers.*

Galatians 6:10

A regular, relaxed Saturday evening in summer of 2009 turned into
our worst nightmare.

Simon and I were driving home from a youth Bible study at
small church in Southern California that we had started attending
a few months prior. We were settling in and making new friends.
As we headed back home that Saturday evening, my husband and
I talked about our plans for the weekend. The green light at the
traffic stop seemed to signal that our lives were going the right way.
We were young and newly married, poised to grow and progress.

Out of nowhere, a sports car rammed into our car on the driver's side. Simon panicked and hit the accelerator, propelling our car
straight into a pole. The air bag deployed. Everything went blank.
The few seconds that followed were at once the loudest and qui-
etest moments of my life. The terrible realization that something
bad had just transpired dawned on me. Still in shock, I felt faint,
exhausted, and confused. Why couldn't I breathe?

I heard my husband's strained voice, "How are you, baby? Are
you OK?"

Music from the Christian radio station in the car played,
undeterred.

I managed to turn my face toward him, my chest still hurting.
I saw fear in his eyes. "I'm OK."

Before we could both figure out how to get out of the car,
firemen landed on the scene. One of them examined me through

the window and assured me he was going to get me out. He cut the seat belt and freed me. Simon was shaken, but he managed to get out of the car by himself.

As a paramedic put me on a stretcher and wheeled me toward the ambulance, I prayed silently, *Thank You, God, that Simon and I are alive. Please help us.*

The ride to the hospital lasted only a few minutes, but my husband stayed close and kept praying as tears trickled down my cheeks nonstop. Over the next few hours, I tried to recollect how the accident happened as the medical staff performed a thorough investigation of my body's reaction to the car crash.

I braced myself for the diagnosis. The reports revealed my sternum suffered a hairline fracture. There was fluid collecting in my lungs, and I needed to be under observation for a few days until I was able to breathe unobstructed again. Morphine and pain meds were pumped into my system to help me cope with the pain. My husband's ribs were bruised. He was in much pain but did not require hospitalization. Like an emergency responder, he threw himself into the task of caring for me, all the while paying little attention to his own pain.

Our lives screeched and halted and toppled over like a crashed car. We had been in America barely a year. We were fresh-off-the-boat immigrants who had no idea how to navigate the American medical system and how to cope with the aftermath of the accident without the help of our families.

But we were not alone. God had provided a small group of friends to support us.

Proxy Family

Within two months of our arrival in Southern California in 2008, we had befriended Louise and her family. Louise spotted us at a church we had visited and ran to us with open arms. Her infectious smile and warm hug made us feel at home.

"I always keep an eye out for Indians like me. I'm so happy to see you both. Welcome to our church."

The next week we celebrated our first Thanksgiving in Louise's

house with her husband, Elias, and two teenage daughters, Saman-
tha and Stephanie. I could tell within a few minutes of meeting
Louise that she was a woman of faith. Her conversations centered
around Jesus—not in a serious, preachy way—but with a lot of
smiling and laughter.

Through Louise, we met Sunita and Stephen who had two
young children under five years of age, Josephine and Joshua. We
bonded with these two families over Indian food, Indian jokes, and
all things Indian. Both families had emigrated from India between
2000 and 2001. They understood the American way of living and
passed on their knowledge to us. Their friendship formed the first
few pieces of straw with which we built a nest of community. We
felt less alone in our new country.

It was no wonder then that we turned to them during our
most difficult time yet as foreigners in America. The first phone
call after the accident was made to Louise. She came to the hospital as soon as she could, held my hand as I cried, read the Bible to
me, and prayed with me. Sunita and Stephen helped Simon pack
a bag for our hospital stay and brought us food. The pastor of our
new church and his wife also came to check in on us. After our
hospital stay ended, Louise opened her house to us for a week so
I could recover.

While our friends in the US went out of their way to support
us in our trial, our family in India felt utterly helpless. They knew
we were suffering but they could not help, soothe, or comfort.
None of them had visas to travel to the US to be with us. However,
they reached out to their relatives and friends in California, many
of whom paid us a visit in the hospital or called to ask how they
could help.

Throughout my time in the hospital, I kept thinking about
how different my situation would have been had I met with an
accident in India. Our parents and siblings would have cared for
us. There wouldn't have been any need to look or ask for help.
Simon and I would not be left alone to wade through a personal
emergency. We would have been enveloped by a circle of loving
care and encouragement.

But in America we were strangers who had to learn how to grieve and cope in isolation. My husband not only had to care for me after we returned to our apartment but also manage insurance, medical, and legal paperwork and issues. My parents helped my sister, Joy, get an emergency visa so that she could come to America to be with me. She arrived almost a month after the incident, but we were greatly comforted by her presence.

Good times do not reveal our need for friendships and fellowship as clearly as bad times. I had never felt more uprooted and upended in my life than in the days following that car crash in 2009. Lack of a support system became my biggest weakness and vulnerability.

Indian Friends

Over the years, as I put down roots in America, I had to make deliberate efforts to make friends and establish a social network. I did this hesitatingly at first since I was almost thirty years old when I set foot in America. I resisted putting myself out there, reaching out to strangers, and starting conversations. But I craved connections.

The craving intensified when I became a mother in 2011. I wanted mommy friends who could relate to me. The apartment complex where we lived at that time had no dearth of young families. And many of them were Indians. Eager and excited, I tried to connect with them.

When I bumped into them in the elevators or in the lobby, I invited them over to my place. I knocked on their doors with home-cooked treats. But I felt my efforts failed. The families did not reciprocate positively. They excluded Ryan and me from their weekly park playdates and did not invite my family to their gatherings.

The Indian families that I failed to bond with were also immigrants like me. They came from different parts of India and were mostly Hindus. I could not help but wonder if they avoided me because I was a Christian. In India, I never experienced discrimination on account of my faith. In fact, all throughout my school and college days, most of my closest friends were either Hindus or Muslims. My circle of Christian friends was small and tight.

In some parts of India, Christians are treated as outsiders. India's caste system has several tiers and layers and is complicated and ancient. Casteism is so systemic that it makes up the fabric of society, both visible and invisible. The rich, powerful, influential, and well-educated Indians represent the upper echelons of the caste system while the economically poor and vulnerable come disproportionately from lower castes. Christians are looked down upon as lower caste citizens, regardless of economic status. While some progress has been made over the years, the evil of casteism is still alive, perpetuated by certain aspects of Hindu philosophy.

Many upper caste Hindus would rather not associate with Christians, forget befriending them. I knew this, in theory. But I had never seen casteism rear its ugly head, explicitly at least, in my time in India. My Hindu friends ate, studied, and danced with me and welcomed me into their homes. My upbringing in Hyderabad had shielded me from experiencing discrimination because of my faith or caste.

But I was shocked and saddened to find that in America my own people did not want to mingle with me because I was a Christian. Ryan and I were left out of sleepovers and birthday parties. And, after repeated attempts to build friendships with my Indian neighbors, I gave up, heartbroken.

Kinds of Friends

One of my closest friends in that apartment building was Jane, whose son was about a year younger than Ryan. I was cooking *dal* in my kitchen one afternoon when I noticed them from the window. Jane was walking in the corridors with her toddler strapped to her back in a sling. The boy's eyes opened and closed as he resisted falling asleep. She waved at me and her boy opened his eyes wide and smiled at me. Something about Jane drew me to her. I invited her and her son inside my house. That was my neighbor's first of many impromptu visits to my small apartment.

We talked about our struggles as mothers and our challenges as immigrants. Our young sons bonded over trains and cars. Our faith in God drew us closer to each other. We enjoyed hanging out in each other's homes for hours. I learned so much about Korean culture and became a fan of Korean food.

As my family moved from one neighborhood to the next, I analyzed my needs for deep connections. Like many immigrants, I needed friendships with other Indians. The yearning for friends who looked like me and belonged to my culture was valid and strong. Indian friends were a bridge between my past and my present. They could relate to my childhood and upbringing in India. They could also understand the adjustments I needed to make to live in America. Making friends with my own kind was comfortable and effortless. I did not have to ask Indians to leave their footwear at the door before entering my home. Nor did I need to explain references to Bollywood actors or Indian food.

But not all good friendships are based on shared ethnic heritage or cultural values. I also welcomed interactions with people from different cultures and backgrounds. I searched for kinship and connection with both immigrants and nonimmigrants. My quest for community made me realize how primal and innate my need was for togetherness and belonging.

Made for Community

After God created Adam, He did not see it fit for him to live alone and fashioned a companion for him. Eve was like Adam, created in God's image, unlike all other creatures. Adam could relate to her and she could understand him. God's blessing to Adam and Eve to be fruitful and multiply (Genesis 1:28) underscores the significance and worth of community. God's plan for mankind included a community of people who were not only individually unique but also corporately similar in their design and function, destined to be His representatives on the planet.

It was not God's intention that human beings live in isolation. Rather, He created us with a need for relationships, partnerships, belonging, and acceptance. We cannot survive on our own, no matter how hard we try. Our life depends on sticking together. The fact that God fashioned us with fingerprint-like, distinctive personalities, strengths, and weaknesses accentuates the importance of our interdependence on one another. We complement one another, we fill up one another's gaps, and we bear one another's burdens.

We are hardwired for community.

Communities are an extension of the family unit. While many of us share our closest bonds with our immediate family members, we also need people outside our families. That's why some of us long to associate with classmates in school or to belong to clubs in college. Our search for our tribe of people makes us join different social circles and online groups. Our network of classmates, neighbors, colleagues, and friends is both a safety net during hard times and a launchpad that propels us forward.

However, our tribes can also become a source of great distress when they hurt us or reject us. The fall has rendered us broken and sinful. Families and communities are not made up of perfect people. Throughout our lives, we grapple with imperfect relationships and uncomfortable social dynamics. Fissures in relationships have the potential to crush our spirits and crumble our identities, but we continue to find and grow meaningful social connections.

An inherent need for community compelled me to rebuild my social network. My friend circle included Indians, Indian Americans, Korean Americans, Armenian Americans, and . . . just Americans. I valued these friendships, acknowledging they were gifts from God, answers to prayer. I found the greatest joy and blessing and the deepest connection in my comradery with friends who shared my faith, regardless of their skin color or ethnic background or nationality.

The body of believers—followers of Christ and citizens of heaven—constitutes the church. And the church is meant to be God's purest and most perfect design for community. We are hardwired not just for community. We are created to serve and glorify God in community and accomplish His purpose on earth together.

The Perfect Family

I recognize that some of us may have been hurt by relationships within the church. We may carry baggage that taints our image of the church or harbor resentment from emotional wounds caused by members of the church or even clergy. A barrage of scandals and scams in recent years may lead us to be skeptical and critical of the church that seems to fall short of our expectations. Some of us may have turned our backs on the church altogether. In fact, our default perception of the church may be that it is a flawed, man-made institution.

But unlike any other faith, club, or organization, the church is more than a community established by men or a group of people coming together for a cause. The church is meant to be one big family. As God's adopted sons and daughters, we are spiritual siblings: "So in Christ Jesus you are all children of God through faith, for all of you who were baptized into Christ have clothed yourselves with Christ" (Galatians 3:26–27).

We worship the same King and we go to the same God for all our needs and wants. Though God is the only one who can satisfy all our needs, He can use our spiritual family to fulfill our desires for acceptance, solidarity, togetherness, and communal purpose. We are bound to each other by the vast love of our heavenly Father who loves us equally, without favoritism (Acts 10:34–36). The Holy Spirit empowers us to lovingly serve one another.

Our ties with our spiritual sisters and brothers can sometimes run deeper than those with our biological families.

When Jesus was told by His disciples that His mother and brothers were waiting to speak to Him, He gave them a reply that was unexpected and unconventional, "He replied to him, 'Who is my mother, and who are my brothers?' Pointing to his disciples, he said, 'Here are my mother and my brothers. For whoever does the will of my Father in heaven is my brother and sister and mother'" (Matthew 12:48–50).

We know from previous accounts in the Gospels that some of Jesus's family members, excluding His mother, neither grasped His true identity nor believed Him at that time (John 7:3–5). Jesus's response indicates that He valued His relationship with His disciples, considering them as important as His relationship with His biological family. He turned the meaning of family upside down. In Jewish culture, family formed an intrinsic part of one's identity.

The family was the most important social unit. So Jesus's followers might have found Jesus's definition of family radical and perplexing.

By redefining family, Jesus laid out a new model for community within the kingdom of God. Anyone who loves God so much that they are willing to lay aside their flesh to yield to God's will, is Jesus's mother, sister, or brother. This new family, with Jesus as its cornerstone, demands our allegiance and attention: "Consequently, you are no longer foreigners and strangers, but fellow citizens with God's people and also members of his household, built on the foundation of the apostles and prophets, with Christ Jesus himself as the chief cornerstone" (Ephesians 2:19–20).

Our love for God drives our commitment to God's people. As citizens of His kingdom, we place our loyalty to Him and, consequently, the church over our loyalty to any other cultural organizations, ethnic associations, or national political parties.

As spiritual siblings, we are called to take care of one another, "Keep on loving one another as brothers and sisters" (Hebrews 13:1). As fellow sojourners, we can support and encourage one another as we anticipate the return of our King, so "Let us consider how we may spur one another on toward love and good deeds . . . encouraging one another—and all the more as you see the Day approaching" (Hebrews 10:24–25).

My Community

The community of God's people is one of the precious gifts that we generously receive when we are saved. This is not an exclusive club with access only to the rich and famous or the educated elite. We come as we are, messy, flawed, and broken. Through an act of faith and because of God's grace, we join God's family, becoming His children forever. We do not have to work to earn our rights and privileges to God's kingdom.

The church can become one of the biggest blessings of our earthly lives.

I became aware of this truth intimately after I became an immigrant. I had taken the church for granted. The absence of a social network in America and the craving for community that was brought on by my travels made me appreciate the beauty and importance of being part of a greater family. God's household is not bound by walls and geographical boundaries. It is also not limited to a certain race or ethnicity or even a denomination. The community of citizens of heaven, consisting of the local as well as the universal church, is spread across the planet.

When Simon and I used to arrive in a new city, one of the first projects we would embark upon was to find a church. The first service in a foreign city bore a special meaning. I did not know anyone in town. Nobody knew me. Many times, my husband and I were the only brown people in the room. But I felt surrounded by family when I worshipped God with other believers, men and women who were strangers but siblings. True, I was a foreigner to them, but we shared the same spiritual genomes, battled against the same enemy, drank from the same streams of Living Water, and ate from the same Bread of Life.

Although my husband and I found it difficult to form deep ties with members from local churches, God was faithful in providing friends outside the church who pointed us to Christ through their love. Our friends belonged to different churches but our common passion for God brought us closer and grew our faith in Him.

When I reflect on the car accident that occurred in 2009, I'm filled with gratitude to God. God preserved my life and provided a group of believers who stood with us through our pain and suffering. And no matter where we lived, Redondo Beach, Torrance, Morristown, Jersey City, Little Rock, Dallas, or San Jose, God has brought brothers and sisters into our lives who have come alongside us as we contend together for our faith.

God's household, the church of the living God, is our constant in the midst of transitions. As "the pillar and foundation of the truth" (1 Timothy 3:15), God's household is our lifeline.

In India, I did not give much thought to the community of citizens of heaven beyond my local church. My experience as an immigrant has opened my eyes to the miracle of community that is the body of believers. I'm amazed to know that I am created to belong to a family prepared for me my God.

I am not alone, even if I'm far away from my biological family and friends in India. I belong to the best community on earth, one that is diverse and widespread and so large that I cannot possibly know how many siblings I have. But I can be certain that I have sisters in China and brothers in Uzbekistan and that through lavish grace of God and the sacrificial blood of Jesus, we are linked together by indissoluble ties.

My immigrant outlook has inspired me to cherishing this heavenly blessing of community. I try to make deliberate efforts to invest in my relationships with my spiritual siblings. I continue to study the Bible weekly with my sisters at Bible Study Fellowship and as often as I can with the women in my church. Every week, I talk over the phone and pray with my writing coach and mentor. We support each other not only in our writing but also in sharing our joys and burdens with each other. My family meets monthly with a few other South Asian families to worship, study the Bible, and pray.

God is also teaching me to be cognizant of the needs of the global church. I pray for countries where persecution is rampant, lamenting over the suffering of my siblings in Christ. I also pray for my brothers and sisters in India, where a nationalist government is clamping down on Christians. Whenever possible, I contribute financially to support missionaries in their endeavor to take God's Word to unreached parts of the world.

A Taste of Heaven

Citizenship in heaven comes with the gift of community, which is powerful and supernatural. Jesus promised that when two or three people gather in His name, He will be present (Matthew 18:20). So whether believers gather on a Sunday morning for church or on a Monday night to watch a movie, we bear His presence, His name. Jesus also said, "Again, truly I tell you that if two of you on earth agree about anything they ask for, it will be done for them by my Father in heaven" (Matthew 18:19). This statement shows the power of the community of kingdom people to bring about change through their connectedness to heaven.

Our love for one another flows from God's love for us and our love for Him: "We love because he first loved us. Whoever claims to love God yet hates a brother or sister is a liar. For whoever does not love their brother and sister, whom they have seen, cannot love God, whom they have not seen. And he has given us this command: Anyone who loves God must also love their brother and sister" (1 John 4:19–21). God's mercy and grace form the cords that bind us together. And the Holy Spirit is the invisible and indivisible force that lends us strength and courage as we come together to overcome suffering and persecution.

Through discipleship and accountability, we are being sanctified even as we spur one another toward holiness, for "in him the whole building is joined together and rises to become a holy temple in the Lord. And in him you too are being built together to become a dwelling in which God lives by his Spirit" (Ephesians 2:21–22). Together, we exist to serve our heavenly Father and glorify Him, on earth and in heaven.

When we come together to declare God's attributes in worship, to learn more about Him through the study His Word, and to petition Him for the needs of our community, we manifest God's presence and power.

The church on earth is a microcosm of heaven, designed to give us a taste of heaven, where we will live with God and with one another for eternity, in perfect love and harmony.

Our identity as sojourners on earth is inextricably linked to our identity as a collective group of God's chosen, holy people who are destined for heaven and devoted to heavenly causes. Our pilgrim paths crisscross, precipitating an interdependence that aligns our hearts and souls with God's. Bound by a singular identity, purpose, and the blood of Jesus, this spectacular spiritual family of God can meet all our needs for community.

Reach In

1. Who are the people you consider to be part of your community?

2. Do you find it challenging to make friends with other Christians? Why?

---

3. What is the most important aspect about community to you?

---

4. How have you been blessed by your friendship and fellowship with other believers?

---

5. When was the last time you thanked God for adopting you into His family and for giving you spiritual siblings?

Reach Out

Share with your family what you learned about God's purpose for His people. Schedule one day in a month when you will invite a family from church to your house for dinner.

Reach Up

Dear Father in Heaven,

I adore You. I am overwhelmed by Your love for me. Thank You for making me Your child. Thank You for sending Your Son to die so that I can live and become a part of Your kingdom. I thank You for the gift of community that You have given to me. You have given me brothers and sisters so I can lean on them and learn from them. So that I may be inspired to press on when the road gets tough. So that I can celebrate my joys and victories with them. Pour out Your love in my heart so I can love my spiritual family. Help me to put their needs ahead of mine and serve them with sincerity. Use me to direct their attention to You and to the secure hope we have in You. Equip me with Your strength and power so that I can work with my fellow citizens to further Your plans on earth.

Amen.

CHAPTER 11
Unity in Diversity

How good and pleasant it is when God's people live together in unity!

Psalm 133:1

I walked into the church prepared to fellowship with other women who were gathering at church that Saturday for a day of prayer. I was eager to participate. The smell of bacon and fresh bread filled the air. I heard laughter. Women chatted with one another in groups as they leisurely partook of the sumptuous breakfast.

I scanned the women to find a darker shade of brown, something I do instinctively when I walk into a white space. I figured I was in the minority. One of the ladies noticed me when I was picking up an empty plate. "Are you new to the church?"

We exchanged introductions and walked toward the food counter as we spoke.

"No, we've been attending this church for about three years. But I've never been to any of the women's events." I picked up some cutlery and paper napkins.

"I'm glad you're here. Let me know if you have any questions." She patted me gently on the back and took leave.

I smiled and nodded as I filled my plate with eggs, bacon, fruit, and bread. I found a round table where two women were talking to one another. I made eye contact with the ladies and joined their table. They smiled at me, and after a few awkward moments of silence, they returned to their conversation. I finished my delicious meal just in time for the prayer to begin.

Everyone walked toward the neatly arranged chairs in front of the stage and took their seats. I settled down in the last row. I had been in the church for only about fifteen minutes, but I felt uncomfortable. As I asked God to check my heart during worship, I concentrated on praising Him with sincerity and gratitude. Then came the prayer time. One by one, a few ladies took the microphone and prayed for different ministries in the church and for the community. The leader directed the women to split into groups of two or three and continue praying.

I shifted in my seat wondering if anyone would join me. I was the only person in my row. I watched as women moved their chairs around into groups of twos and threes. Was I invisible? My brightly colored top and winged eyeliner, not to mention my brown skin, made me stand out in this group. Should I ask to join a group? I couldn't muster the courage to ask a group if I could join. Their body language suggested they had no space for me.

So I remained in my seat, feeling like I didn't belong. Putting my thoughts aside, I prayed solo for the needs of the church. When the time of prayer ended, I did not want to make eye contact with any of the ladies. A sense of urgency to leave took over me. I exited the doors before the closing worship song.

I never again attended any events organized by the women of that church. Although I do not believe the ladies in the group deliberately decided to exclude me like playground bullies, I felt unwanted and ignored.

We Need a Church

As an immigrant who has visited or been part of many churches in America, I have experienced firsthand the reaction of many of these churches to foreigners or foreign-looking attendees. I've discovered that discrimination and exclusion happen more often than not in subtle ways, through actions and inaction, rather than words.

My family has been part of at least five churches in America. Because we moved around a lot, our time in each church varied from a few months to four years. Some churches had built a culture of acceptance into their model of worship and fellowship. They were thoughtful and consistent about welcoming newcomers and including outsiders into the fold. But other churches failed to foster an atmosphere where minorities or people of color felt included.

Still, my husband and I believed in the power of the local church and knew we needed a church family.

When we pitched our tent in a new city, we made it our first priority to look for a church. Simon and I were born and raised in Indian Christian homes where church-going was emphasized as a spiritual discipline and the church community was viewed as extended family. During our childhood and youth, we were involved in church not just as Sunday service congregants but also as helpers, volunteers, and ministry leaders. Long-term friend-ships within the church helped us learn about God and grow in faith alongside others in a safe environment. Our roots in the local church ran deep and strong.

My husband and I set out to find, in America, what we had left behind and so desperately desired to regain—a church family. We looked for lively worship, the uncompromising teaching of God's Word, and a welcoming community. We longed, also, to be part of a congregation that consisted of young families like ours.

We used more or less the same methodology while checking out churches in every city. We searched the internet for churches nearby, visited church websites to see if their statement of faith aligned with our values, and asked neighbors and friends for recom-mendations. We drew up plans to visit one church every Sunday. Prayer helped us make a final decision. In His providence, God led us to the churches that He had planned for our family.

The first church Simon and I visited in America when we arrived in 2008 in Southern California was a small church near the hotel where we had been staying. The majority of the congregants were senior citizens and white. But we enjoyed singing hymns with them and found the sermon uplifting. Getting our first taste of church outside our homeland proved to be more emotional than I had realized.

Throughout the service I fought hard to stem the flow of tears. My heart ached when I thought of my home church. After the ser-vice, the congregants were so eager to meet us and know our story that we almost felt like VIPs. They were unaware of the emotional rollercoaster that I was experiencing, but their friendly and cheerful nature soothed me.

We did not settle down with this church family because we were looking for a congregation that was closer to our age, but this church still holds a special place in our hearts.

Alienated

Over the years, we hoped to find friendships, fellowship, and family in the local churches. However, for the most part, we did not. Though people in the church did not explicitly treat us unkindly, I felt the pressure to prove that I belonged, that I was a genuine believer, and that I was American enough. Most churches gave me the impression that I was an alien who needed to stay outside the circle. They couldn't trust my unfamiliar Christian upbringing or cultural background.

I have become used to people showing surprise at my *good* English, but I am appalled when my knowledge of the Bible and understanding of biblical truths elicit raised eyebrows in church circles. Some people assume that I am behind by default. They assume that I have more to learn from them than I have to offer. They assume that Christianity, like English, is my second language. They assume that my Indian Christianity is lesser than their American Christianity.

At one particular church, I volunteered to help with the church's youth group. I shared with the leader of the youth ministry my heart for young people and offered to lend a hand wherever help was needed. She nodded her head without saying a word. I felt dismissed. After a few weeks, the pastor of the church approached to ask if I could help with the website design of the church. He thought, like many Americans, that Indians were proficient in all things that concerned computers, and apparently, web design. I told him I had zero knowledge about how to maintain a website but I would be happy to learn and assist my church family wherever there was a need.

One of the reasons some American believers treat believers from non-Western countries as second-class congregants is probably because many believe Christianity is a Western religion. This belief is ludicrous because Jesus was a Middle Eastern Jew. The twelve disciples and early followers of Christ who laid the foundation for the church came from the East. While it is true that missionaries and colonizers from the West transplanted Christianity to many parts of Asia and Africa, it does not imply that there were no Christians on these continents before the arrival of Westerners. Some of the oldest Christian communities can be found in Egypt, Ethiopia, Syria, Iraq, and even India.

Ethnic Churches and Gatherings

A few well-meaning friends ask if I go to an Indian church. I understand the reasons behind this question. They may believe that I would want to worship with people from my culture in my language. After all, there are thousands of Chinese and Korean churches in America where members worship in their native tongue and form strong ties with one another since they share the same culture. However, Indian churches are few and far between since Indians are not a homogenous group like some other Asians.

India is home to hundreds of subcultures. My husband and I come from two different states in India. Our families speak different languages, enjoy different cuisines, and also follow different traditions. Moreover, Christians constitute a small minority of Indian immigrants. Small churches in America that cater to particular Indian subcultures do exist but they are uncommon.

The first Indian church my husband and I visited was a church that catered mainly to Telugus and met on Sunday evenings in New Jersey. Telugus, like me, hail from the states of Telangana and Andhra Pradesh in India. The church service was bilingual, in English and Telugu. After the service, there was a lavish spread of Indian food for dinner. The women wore saris. The conversation switched between English and Telugu effortlessly. My husband and I enjoyed the company of the cheerful bunch of Indian immigrants (despite the fact that Simon does not understand or speak Telugu).

For most members, this church was not their primary church. They also attended a mainline church on Sunday mornings. It is quite common among Indian immigrants to attend more than one church during the week—one mainline church and the other, an ethnic church. Or they belonged to an association or some kind of gathering of ethnic Christians that met regularly through an informal Bible study or a formal church gathering. My family visited one such gathering in Silicon Valley that met monthly. This one, too, was meant for Telugus. We worshipped the Lord together through English and Telugu songs and got to know other families through food and fellowship after the service. Connecting with my Telugu brothers and sisters who shared my Christian roots brought me great joy and relief.

From interacting with other Indian immigrants, I've observed that some of us attend mainline churches even though we struggle to establish close friendships; we attempt to blend in and hope to be accepted. We fall back on the ethnic churches or ethnic Christian gatherings not only to stay connected to our cultural roots but also to fill the void of genuine community.

This is especially true for my family. My ministry with Bible Study Fellowship opened the doors to meaningful friendships that I somehow failed to cultivate in the local church. Barriers of culture and race somehow seemed to disappear in this nondenominational parachurch organization. The Los Angeles class of BSF that I was a part of for six years was a diverse family of all races—African Americans, Hispanics, Chinese, Korean, Filipino, and others. I blended in, though I was one of two Indian women in this group of about three hundred women, since I had much in common with other members. One other reason could be that we gathered consistently every week, in small groups, to study the Bible and share our learnings with one another.

I am aware that such organizations are not churches and cannot stand in for the local church. But BSF became a source of spiritual nourishment and community for me. And so did our network of Indian Christian friends who all went to different churches but came together to celebrate holidays and important family events. We have also been able to form strong bonds with parents of my son's friends who attend the same Christian schools. Our family came to rely on this network of immigrant and non-immigrant Christian friends for support and friendship. In the absence of families, these friends stepped in to fill the gap, becoming our proxy families.

Nevertheless, I never gave up on asking God to graft us into a church where faith and family can come together to make it our home. God did not disappoint. His answer came in 2019 when my family moved to San Jose, California. After months of searching, God led us to a church which felt like home within minutes of walking inside.

The diversity seen in this multiethnic church lay not just in the optics but in the way congregants were involved with one another's lives and worshipped together. For the first time in several years, I never felt I was an outsider in this group. My family is starting to make more and more connections within this body of believers.

Diversity in the Church

Viewing the local church only as a source of spiritual food but not community negates the original purpose and design for the church. But many minorities and people of color will continue to adopt this model unless churches actively promote and support diversity.

My desire is to see local churches become spiritual hubs where people from a variety of cultures and backgrounds find home and belonging. Unity with diversity is the future that the apostle John envisioned for the people of God in Revelation 7:9–10, "After this I looked, and behold, a great multitude that no one could number, from every nation, from all tribes and peoples and languages, standing before the throne and before the Lamb, clothed in white robes, with palm branches in their hands, and crying out with a loud voice, 'Salvation belongs to our God who sits on the throne, and to the Lamb!'" (ESV).

Diversity is built into our identity as citizens of God's kingdom. A close examination of the foundation of our faith will reveal that diversity is embodied in the very design of the church.

Jesus was, in all probability, a brown man with dark hair. But Jesus did not come to earth to draw attention to his skin color or looks. Rather, Jesus came to usher in the kingdom of God and mediate the new covenant through His sacrificial death on the cross. He came to save us all, both Jew and Gentile, and to grant us free citizenship to His kingdom. He came to break down walls so that people of all skin colors and nationalities can be reconciled to God and have access to heavenly riches.

Jesus gave His life so that people from all cultures and nations can become one family under His leadership and rule,

And they sang a new song, saying:

"You are worthy to take the scroll
    and to open its seals,
because you were slain,
    and with your blood you purchased for God
    persons from every tribe and language and people and
      nation."

(Revelation 5:9)

Salvation is the great equalizer and unifier. It eliminates hierarchy or status within the kingdom of God. We enjoy equal privileges and rights as children of God and citizens of His kingdom. There is no place for favoritism. The apostle Paul explains that we are all parts of one body, with each part playing a significant role in the building up of the church (1 Corinthians 12:12–27).

God created each of us with a distinct set of skills, endowing diversity even within a single race. But we are all equal, equally loved and valued by God. We may be differently abled and look different, but there are no superior or inferior parts.

Regarding unity in the church, the apostle Paul wrote, "For just as the body is one and has many members, and all the members of the body, though many, are one body, so it is with Christ. For in one Spirit we were all baptized into one body—Jews or Greeks, slaves or free—and all were made to drink of one Spirit" (1 Corinthians 12:12–13 ESV). Paul is implying that we do not have to go out of our way to generate or manufacture unity. Our salvation and baptism in the Holy Spirit unify us as one body. We have to put to death not only our old selves but also the divisions and discords that accompanied our sinful nature. Our new identity in Christ includes oneness and equality with our brothers and sisters.

Paul called out the way the Corinthian Christians fostered a culture of division. At the time of Paul's writings, the Lord's Supper, the partaking of bread and wine in remembrance of Christ's sacrifice, was part of a communal meal. While the rich Corinthians indulged themselves and ate heartily, the poor left hungry. The apostle decried the divisive nature of their gatherings, "Don't you have homes to eat and drink in? Or do you despise the church of God by humiliating those who have nothing? What shall I say to you? Shall I praise you? Certainly not in this matter!" (1 Corinthians 11:22).

By humiliating the poor, the Corinthians despised the church. When we belittle, insult, dismiss, or alienate the poor, the marginalized, the foreigner, and believers from different races, we show contempt for the church, the body of Christ. When we look down on our Hispanic brother sitting next to us in the church pew or think less of our Chinese sister handing out church bulletins, we disrespect God. When we give more prominence to the rich or the well-educated than others, we dishonor God. Discrimination of any kind fractures the church and minimizes Christ's work on the cross.

I believe it grieves God's heart when He sees racism and xenophobia rear their ugly heads in His family because God is the source of diversity. Our Creator deliberately fashioned human beings in different colors and shades. Just like the mountains, seas, moon, and stars, we, too, were created to reflect God's beauty and creative power. The function of the body of Christ is not to make everything and everyone uniform by erasing differences but to embrace diversity and view it as a seedbed for strength and unity and harmony.

Unity in the Church

Paul's exhortation to the Corinthian church to be "perfectly united in mind and thought" (1 Corinthians 1:10) echoes Jesus's prayer for unity among His followers. Jesus's prayer sets a high bar for unity by pointing to the unity in diversity embodied in the Triune God as a model for oneness among His disciples, "I have given them the glory that you gave me, that they may be one as we are one—I in them and you in me—so that they may be brought to complete unity. Then the world will know that you sent me and have loved them even as you have loved me" (John 17:22–23). Just as God the Father, God the Son, and God the Holy Spirit are one, we, too, must be perfectly joined together in our thoughts, words, and actions.

Jesus's prayer also demonstrates the purpose and power of a church that is united. When the world sees harmony and love in a diverse body of believers, they will be drawn to the gospel. They will know God's love for them through the witness of the church. Each local church is supposed to be a testimony to the love and power and glory of God. The local church must embody the gospel.

The goal of unity, and hence diversity, is to declare God's goodness to the world. How wonderful it will be if the world looked at the church as a representation of God's love, a model for diversity with communal harmony and equality!

Sadly, the reality is far from ideal or perfect. Too many churches fail to live up to God's standards for unity. Discrimination on the basis of gender, race, ethnic background, socioeconomic status, age, and education level exists in the body of Christ. It is not possible to completely get rid of bigotry and partiality, because we are sinners who will make mistakes. But we can ask the Holy Spirit to help us identify and root out prejudices of all sorts and relentlessly pursue peace. We must take the mandate of sustaining our Christ-centered unity seriously, "Make every effort to keep the unity of the Spirit through the bond of peace" (Ephesians 4:3).

Plank in My Eye

My experiences as an outsider in American churches have made me reflect on how I treat others who are different from me. The Holy Spirit convicts me when sometimes I assume certain things about a certain group of people or when I favor some people over others.

Born and raised in India, I grew up in a society that normalized casteism and racism. Most Indians prefer light skin to dark skin, and associate darker skin with a lower status. In many cases, women with a darker skin tone have a difficult time getting married, as men want to marry fairer women. I was also raised in an environment where one's socioeconomic level determined one's status in the community. These cultural messages can impact how I interact with others.

Like almost every middle-class family, my family in India employed domestic help to assist with our household chores. Known as servants, these women came from poorer families and were also either less educated or entirely uneducated. Most Indian families treat them kindly, but they also show them *their place* by not allowing them to sit on furniture or share meals with them at the same table. Even in my own house, separate cups, plates, and cutlery were assigned to servants, as though our household items would be contaminated if they used them.

I was raised in a Christian family, yet cultural values seeped into me unnoticed, shaping my worldview. God's gentle but vivid rebuke came to me one day when I least expected it.

I had just given birth to Ryan and was living with my mother in India. Early one morning, around four o'clock, the baby's cries woke me up. With eyes half opened, I changed my infant's diaper and settled down in a chair as I began feeding him. The bedroom door was ajar. I did not bother to shut it completely since I knew nobody would be up so early. Nobody but the maid. This maid had been my mother's employee for several years. She had been living with us for the past few weeks to help us care for the baby. She was also a Christian.

Through the slight opening in the door, I saw her kneeling down in the kitchen, her hair covered with her saree (some Christians in India believe women should cover their heads while praying) and her hands folded. I had known that she woke up early to pray every day, but this was the first time I witnessed it. My sleepy eyes widened as I heard God's message loud and clear in my heart, "She is mine. She is precious in my sight. And I love her as much as I love you."

This maid was uneducated. She had come to know the Lord only by hearing the Word. She could not read the Bible. But she attended prayer meetings and church gatherings where the Bible was preached, hanging on to every word of the preachers and teachers. God impressed on my heart that day that though the Indian society accorded her the lowest status, in His kingdom, she was most favored. She was my sister in Christ. She was not my servant. She was His servant, and so was I.

Love and Unity

I cannot pick and choose whom to love. God's command to love my neighbor rules out excuses and biases. My neighbor may not look like me or dress like me. My neighbor may speak in a foreign language. My neighbor may be poor, wearing torn clothes. But I am commanded to look past the differences that exist between me and my neighbor and choose to love. I must not only recognize the commonalities but appreciate them, seeing them as solid reasons to embrace my neighbor.

The things we have in common with our fellow citizens are spiritual in nature, unseen but true. We are often misled by our eyes to see the external, the skin color, and perhaps the clothes. Our ears hear an unfamiliar language that may not sound sweet or musical. Our minds are influenced by the world, which tells us to either ignore or welcome someone based on secular standards. Yet, as people who live in between the seen and the unseen, the earthly and the eternal, we are called to put on a spiritual vision and see the other as a brother, a sibling gifted to us by our Father and King.

The more I think about some of the problems I had with some American churches, the more I'm convinced that all those experiences were part of God's lesson plan to teach me to keep an eye out for the ones kept at the periphery of church circles. I know what it means to feel unwelcome and excluded. There are Christians like me who, sadly, are living in the hope that a day will come when, maybe, someone will see them as equal and treat them fairly.

My experiences have challenged me to identify attitudes that cause me to differentiate among believers, classifying them as those who deserve my attention and those that do not. As I pray for churches to be more welcoming, I also pray that I can root out sinful patterns of behavior and learn to love others with the love of Jesus.

My desire is to see the body of Christ unified, embracing and encouraging diversity. Pursuing oneness is inconvenient, requiring reserves of humility and courage that we cannot possibly find in ourselves. But we can tap into the inexhaustible supply of spiritual resources available to us as citizens of heaven and trust that God will show us the way.

Unity with diversity is not optional. It is an essential part of our identity and calling as citizens of heaven. And since that kind of Spirit-inspired and Spirit-based unity can only be a product of godly love, our unity can be a visible representation of God's love to the world, a shadow of heaven on earth.

Reach In

1. When was the last time you felt like a stranger in a church setting?

_____

2. How will you praise and thank God today for the diversity you see in your church?

_____

3. How have you been blessed by a diverse body of believers?

_____

4. Who are your closest friends inside and outside the church? How can you go out of your way to include in your friend circle someone who does not look like you or someone who you consider different?

_____

5. What prejudices do you battle within your heart that keep you from loving a particular group or groups of people?

_____

Reach Out

Write a letter of thanks to someone who extended their hand of friendship to you when you were new to a church or a community of believers. Recall specific events or words that made you feel welcome and connected.

Reach Up

Dear Father in Heaven,

Thank You for creating me in Your image. I know You love me just the way I am. Give me Your eyes so I can see my brothers and sisters the way You see them and love them. Show me how to root out biases in my heart and convict me when I show partiality. May I have compassion in my heart especially for the misfits, the outcasts, the poor, and the marginalized. Inspire me to intentionally cultivate friendships with those who do not look like me. May I glorify You in my relationships with my fellow citizens.

Amen.

CONCLUSION
Moving Forward

March 2020

COVID happened. As the virus traversed borders and crossed oceans, a tragedy of huge proportions rocked the world. Fear and uncertainty gripped several nations. The coronavirus brought with it pain, grief, and death. Separating ourselves from friends and family became an essential tool for survival at a time when, ironically, the need to be close to our loved ones was never stronger. The world as we knew it became unrecognizable and so dangerous to our health that staying locked up at home was the safest thing to do.

California was one of the first states in the US to go into lockdown. In the beginning of March, my husband was asked to work from home by his organization. All of Silicon Valley went virtual, abandoning huge, fancy office spaces. Children were sent home from school and told not to return until further notice. Restaurants, retail outlets, movie theaters, libraries, and churches shut down. Social gatherings were canceled. We had to stay put with our families in our homes.

Our lives turned upside down and came to a painful halt.

The virus did not show mercy to anyone, infecting the rich and the poor, the strong and the weak, the young and the old, and the believer and the unbeliever alike. It did not even spare leaders of powerful nations. And it was especially brutal to the vulnerable among us, senior citizens and those with underlying health conditions.

Grappling for more information, health officials, scientists, and government leaders all over the world initially operated in the dark. They could not make any assurances or promises to the public. The only thing they were sure of was that we were in the midst of a pandemic. Quarantining ourselves was crucial to curb the spread of the illness. This virus was worse than the flu. Our bodies had not developed an immunity to the novel coronavirus since we had never been exposed to this strain of virus. A vaccine was not available. A treatment plan or cure was unknown. We watched in horror as the number of infected people and the death toll in America and elsewhere started to rise.

May 2020

Just as we started to adjust to the terrible, unwelcome normal brought on by the pandemic, racial tensions in America reached a peak. Incensed by some incidents of police brutality against African Americans, many Americans took to the streets to condemn racism and demand justice. Communities of color lamented the injustice they had been suffering and voiced their frustrations with institutional racism. While a few protests turned violent, most were peaceful, sparking a national debate about racial reconciliation in America.

Conversations about race, inequality, and discrimination dominated television, radio, social media, and almost everything on the internet, causing a great awakening about race relations in America on a scale that was unprecedented in recent history.

July 2020

Here in California, we were still catching a breath when record-breaking wildfires swept through the state in summer, lasting into fall. Approximately four million acres of land burned, making the 2020 wildfire season the largest in California's modern history. Thousands of people were forced to evacuate. Houses and businesses were ablaze. The fire displaced many families. Lives were lost.

November 2020

This was also the year of the US presidential elections. Divisions between political parties and their supporters grew deeper in an already polarized America. In some cases, differences of opinion about politics separated close friends and even family members. Sadly, the elections also caused fissures within the Christian community.

When I look back at 2020, I cannot help but feel it was a nightmare of sorts. It seemed as though terrible and tragic events kept piling on without end. Sometimes, I wondered what else was coming for us. What catastrophe was going to strike us next? We got pummeled by so much bad news that it was not easy to keep joy and hope alive.

Most of this book was written during the year 2020. I believed God timed the writing of the book to coincide with world events. I think He wanted to challenge me to live out the truths I had been writing about. I asked myself how my identity as a spiritual immigrant on earth helped me navigate the tumultuous events of 2020.

I started this book by talking about how change can trigger an identity crisis. That was the problem I tried to tackle in the first chapter of this book. The pandemic, surely, must have had an effect on our identity as the citizens of God's kingdom, both individually and corporately.

God Is with Us, Always

When quarantine was imposed on us in March 2020, I assumed it would last a few weeks. So, I braced myself for a temporary adjustment. I thought it would not be a big deal to stop seeing my friends, shopping at stores, attending church and Bible study, going to the movies, or inviting friends to my house.

As weeks turned into months, I felt as if my wings had been clipped. I wanted to fly, but I couldn't. I am a social person. Not having face-to-face interactions with people started to make me feel lonely. It took me back to my first few days in America. I did not know anyone when I landed in Southern California more than a decade ago. Days and weeks had passed without talking and laughing with friends. I recall loathing the silence that echoed in the walls of our apartment. Although I used to speak with my family and friends in India over the phone, I remember those initial days as being marked by intense loneliness and a deep sadness.

Memories of my isolated life in 2008 made me empathize with people who wrestled with quarantine during the pandemic. A few of my friends welcomed not having social interactions, but many others did not enjoy being confined to their homes. Living alone compounded loneliness for some people. I did my best to reach out to them over the phone and check in on them.

Sheltering in place made me reflect on my journey with Jesus. I reminisced about my past and saw how God used circumstances in my life both in India and America to mature my faith. The same God who was with me as a new immigrant and helped me go through the storms of migration is the God who could help me deal with the frustrations of being quarantined.

God's faithfulness remains unchanged, through all seasons and circumstances. His presence never leaves me, as the psalmist expresses,

> Where can I go from your Spirit?
>> Where can I flee from your presence?
> If I go up to the heavens, you are there;
>> if I make my bed in the depths, you are there.
> If I rise on the wings of the dawn,
>> if I settle on the far side of the sea,
> even there your hand will guide me,
>> your right hand will hold me fast.
>
> (Psalm 139:7–10)

We can count on God's unchanging friendship when we experience loneliness. I learned that the quarantine may have distanced me from my friends and loved ones, but it could not distance me from God. I got the chance, in fact, to spend more time with Him and grow closer to Him.

God Has a Purpose

The pandemic, no doubt, turned my world upside down. Like many others, I had a hard time dealing with the changes.

I love spending time with my family but sometimes I wish my husband and son were not home all the time. On one hand, I disliked social distancing, while on the other hand, I lamented the loss of my privacy and space. The boundaries between work and family blurred, causing stress to freely circulate inside the house. When one of us exploded, all of us did . . . almost. Concentrating on writing became difficult for me as the house was abuzz with activity and the list of household chores was never ending.

But God was gracious in gently nudging me to see things differently. I began to ask myself what God's will was for me in these unique circumstances. He urged me to place the needs of others before mine. Had I been paying too much attention to my own wants and desires? The pandemic made life inconvenient for me. I resisted sacrificing my comfort to care for my small family.

I sought God's guidance on how I could nurture and support my family during the quarantine, and He did not disappoint. God recalibrated my thinking. I did not become a perfect wife and mother overnight. However, I became more conscious of the fact that I could make a difference in the lives of my husband and son through my words and actions, particularly during a stressful time. My husband was dealing with a few problems of his own at work. Online learning was new to my son, who missed going to school and playing outside in a park.

With God's help, I tried to support Simon and Ryan as they coped with the changes. I wanted to create a joyful, peaceful, and harmonious environment at home. This led me to rely on God daily for sustenance, strength, and wisdom to care for my family. My God-given purpose was to serve God by taking care of the emotional and physical needs of my family.

The global health crisis of 2020 affected almost everyone everywhere in the world, including me. I was not immune to fear and worry. But the pressures of 2020 neither weakened my thread of faith nor shattered my identity. They made me cling to God, who protected me and took care of me. He was patient with me, overlooked my weaknesses, even using them to manifest His strength.

God also challenged me to live out my faith by ministering to those who were adversely impacted by the pandemic.

God Sends Us

Prayer was my first and immediate response when I saw rates of infection increase. Throughout my life, I have felt called to intercede for people, particularly when there is a largescale calamity. I believe in the heavenly power of prayer to change things and alleviate suffering in the world.

But God also wants us to practically demonstrate His love to others, out of love for Him. God commands us to love our neighbors. This is the purpose of our earthly pilgrimage, not a legalistic requirement of the Christian faith.

Our compassionate actions toward others are evidence of our love for God. This is the reason why James declares that faith without works is dead, "Suppose a brother or a sister is without clothes and daily food. If one of you says to them, 'Go in peace; keep warm and well fed,' but does nothing about their physical needs, what good is it? In the same way, faith by itself, if it is not accompanied by action, is dead" (James 2:15–17).

During quarantine, in the early months of 2020, I was glued to the television when the news of a global health crisis broke. I saw people dying alone in hospitals, far from their loved ones. Some families lost their breadwinners. Doctors, nurses, and healthcare professionals were overwhelmed and overworked. Many people lost their jobs and struggled to pay rent and other bills. Children from families of low income suffered disproportionately, as they lacked laptops or reliable internet service for online learning. Working parents had to work from home while also supervising their children's online schooling.

The more I thought about the state of affairs, the sadder I got. I could not keep the grief and pain of those around me from making their way into my heart and soul. I prayed for guidance as to how I could be God's hands and feet, recognizing that I am His representative on earth. I could not sit around and do nothing.

When I decided to volunteer at a local food bank, some of my friends thought I was being rash by risking my health and my family's well-being. They asked why I was deliberately putting myself in harm's way. I must admit that their comments made me nervous and fearful of the virus. What if my family got sick because of me?

I discovered that self-preservation, beyond a point, could end up being a hindrance to carrying out God's command to love others. I was reminded of a friend in India who shared with me that some doctors in the hospital where she worked resigned while a few others called in sick because they did not want to risk contracting the virus. The idea of healthcare workers shirking their duties at such a crucial time troubled me.

As God's children on earth, we are the frontline workers in God's army. It is incumbent upon us to respond to an emergency or tragedy in our neighborhood or community with love in action. The pandemic was a national and international emergency. We are called "for such a time as this" (Esther 4:14) to show up and serve others. We are a people uniquely equipped by the Holy Spirit and sent by God to bring light to the dark places. We are not just the *chosen* ones. We are the *sent* ones.

I'm not saying I abandoned all fear of the virus. Some fear, common sense tells us, is a good thing. Healthy fear causes us to take precautions like wearing masks, sanitizing hands, and maintaining social distance. But I had to balance that fear with faith. I volunteered at the food bank, believing that I was doing what God sent me to do and that He would not only equip me to carry out His will but also protect me and my family. I also helped deliver groceries to an elderly friend.

The pandemic was a wake-up call for me. It forced me to consider the Great Commandment seriously,

Jesus replied: "'Love the Lord your God with all your heart and with all your soul and with all your mind.' This is the first and greatest commandment. And the second is like it: 'Love your neighbor as yourself.' All the Law and the Prophets hang on these two commandments." (Matthew 22:37–40)

The global crisis made me recognize that loving others meant laying down my rights for the sake of others. Wearing a mask was inconvenient. Not being able to entertain friends in my house was no fun. And I missed gathering with other believers to worship God. But I discovered that sacrificing these comforts and even necessities was crucial so that we could curb the virus's spread and protect the most vulnerable members of our communities. My inconvenience was a small price to pay for the sake of others' safety.

God Is in Control

The pandemic also brought into focus the frailty and brevity of human lives. As much as we marvel at the genius of the human mind and put our confidence in the power of science to help fight disease, we were humbled by the realization that we were nearly powerless against an unknown enemy. Scientists took time to catch up with the coronavirus, and by the time a vaccine was manufactured and administered, hundreds of thousands of lives were lost.

We are not only weak and fragile but also mortal, with no control over our destinies. Our pilgrimage on earth is temporary and in God's control. Psalm 90:5–6 captures the essence of our transitory presence on earth,

> Yet you sweep people away in the sleep of death—
> they are like the new grass of the morning:
> In the morning it springs up new,
> but by evening it is dry and withered.

The psalmist compares God's immortality with our own mortality, "Teach us to number our days, that we may gain a heart of wisdom" (v. 12).

We need godly wisdom to have the right perspective on the brevity of our earthly pilgrimage so that we discharge our duties as Christ's ambassadors without getting tangled up in the affairs of the world but channeling our attention toward heavenly purposes. Keeping our immigrant identity at the front and center of our lives reminds us to number our days. To consider how each day can be spent in our Lord's service. To view each day as a gift from God to be cherished. To see each day as an opportunity to witness God's hand at work in our lives and in the world around us.

If we know that our lives can be taken away at any moment, then we need to consider our attitude also toward death, and maintaining an eternal perspective helps us form a proper view of death.

Death is not the end of the road for individuals who have accepted Jesus as their Savior. Death is not a closed door. Rather, it opens the door to live the richest and fullest life we could possibly imagine, forever. The demise of our earthly bodies transports our souls into the presence of our King. We will behold the face of our Lord and Savior and feast in the abundance of His love in heaven. We need not worry about the loved ones we leave behind since God will take care of them. He loves them more than we do and His plans for them are good. So, we lose nothing when we die. We gain much, whether we die young or old, whether we die from the coronavirus or from natural causes.

When we grasp the hope of the future we have in Christ, we can be less fearful of death, viewing it as an entryway to our glorious, eternal home with Him. We can entrust our earthly journey to God, believing that our future is secure in His mighty, able hands.

The year 2020 was a whirlwind of a year. But God taught me to rely on His faithfulness, believe He is in control, and trust in His purpose for me. I also learned that He wants me to be the salt and light of the earth, focusing on how I can love by showing His love to others.

These truths help me move forward and face my future with confidence in Him.

Readiness for the Future

I do not know what catastrophe might hit our world next, but I believe I can be ready for the future by choosing to walk with Jesus one day and one moment at a time. I do not have to live in fear of the next tragedy, but I can rely on God daily to build my faith so that He can enable me to stand firm in faith and persevere through suffering. He can use me to help others get through their trials when the opportunity beckons. Every moment I spend with God now supplies me with the spiritual power I need for the next day. Today's circumstances can be a training ground for tomorrow's battles.

Many nations admitted that they were ill-equipped to handle a health emergency of large proportions. They did not have the infrastructure and emergency systems in place to tackle a contagion like the coronavirus. I could not help but wonder if the church was prepared for the impacts of the global health crisis and other events of 2020. I do not think many churches in America were ready for uncomfortable conversations and decisions involving race and unity.

But we can certainly learn from the pressures we encountered in 2020 and be better prepared for tomorrow's events.

The racial tensions in America have awakened the conscience of many churches all over the country. We can lay a solid foundation for the future by resolving to pursue unity and peace and championing diversity in the body of Christ. God can help us put aside our egos so that we can humbly take the first step toward understanding the frustrations of the minorities in our community. He can show us the path toward reconciliation and healing.

A united church is better equipped to deal with the pressures of pandemics, natural disasters, and political and racial tensions.

Only history will reveal the extent of the impact the church had on healing the divides between different races in America as well as on coping with the repercussions of the pandemic. But I know that the events of 2020 revealed our need to come together as the spiritual family of God. When one of us hurts, we all feel the pain since we are connected by the blood of Jesus.

Political parties or presidents are not the basis for our unity. The color of our skin or our nationality are also not the reasons for us to stick together. We cannot perceive ourselves primarily as Republicans, Democrats, Indians, Mexicans, Americans, Black, or White. We are first and foremost children of God, followers of Jesus, and citizens of the kingdom of God. This core identity pulls us closer and keeps our attention on Jesus, His people and His kingdom. This identity enables us to come together to reach out to those who are hurting and tell them about Jesus.

We are immigrants on earth.

God knows all the details of our pilgrimage and He has a purpose for our journey. He promises to go with us and ahead of us. Even in our imperfect human form, we can experience the joy of walking and talking with God every day, taking part in His grand plans for humanity. And He will preserve us and lead us to the home He has prepared for us.

APPENDIX 1

Love Your Immigrant Neighbor: Action Plan for Individuals

Recent world events have brought immigration to the forefront of public discourse and the socioeconomic and political agendas of countries across the world. The United Nations estimates that there are more than 250 million international migrants in the world.[1] In the United States alone, there are fifty million first-generation immigrants—close to 15 percent of the country's population.

While there has been a surge in negative attitudes and hateful rhetoric toward immigrants and refugees in recent years, many Christians are rising to Jesus's call to care for the stranger:

> Then the King will say to those on his right, "Come, you who are blessed by my Father; take your inheritance, the kingdom prepared for you since the creation of the world. For I was hungry and you gave me something to eat, I was thirsty and you gave me something to drink, I was a stranger and you invited me in, I needed clothes and you clothed me, I was sick and you looked after me, I was in prison and you came to visit me." (Matthew 25:34–36).

Jesus clarifies that serving the poor, the sick, and the foreigner is a natural outcome of our love for Him and identifies us as His true followers, "The King will reply, 'Truly I tell you, whatever you

---

[1] United Nations Department of Economic & Social Affairs, *International Migration Report 2017*.

did for one of the least of these brothers and sisters of mine, you did for me'" (Matthew 25:40).

Kindness to foreigners was also emphasized in the Old Testament as one of the requirements of God's people, "For the LORD your God is God of gods and Lord of lords, the great God, mighty and awesome, who shows no partiality and accepts no bribes. He defends the cause of the fatherless and the widow, and loves the foreigner residing among you, giving them food and clothing. And you are to love those who are foreigners, for you yourselves were foreigners in Egypt" (Deuteronomy 10:17–19).

Here are a few tips on how you can reach out to your neighbor, friend, or a member in your church who is an immigrant:

- Pray for God to give you opportunities to minister to foreigners. Seek out immigrants in your circles. Keep an eye out for those who are new to your city or church.

- Ask questions and get to know immigrants.

- Do some research about their country and culture.

- When you welcome a new family to your neighborhood, give them useful information about the area. Connect them with other immigrant families in the neighborhood. Give them your phone number so they can reach out to you. Check in on them frequently.

- Don't wait for an opportunity to connect.

- Invite them to your house and introduce your family to theirs.

- Look for special occasions to bless them.

- Many people are unsure of what to say and do for fear of causing unintended hurt. Don't be afraid to make mistakes. Most immigrants will overlook your errors and appreciate your efforts to bond with them.

APPENDIX 2

Love Your Immigrant Neighbor: Action Plan for Churches

- Preach on kindness to foreigners from the pulpit at least once a year. It sends a message that loving your immigrant neighbors is biblical, not political. The rhetoric about immigrants and refugees is becoming more and more hateful these days. It is important that churches combat these messages through solid biblical preaching. It also demonstrates the commitment of your church toward the cause.

- Be aware of the makeup of your community. What is the demographic of immigrants and refugees in and around your church? Are they predominantly from a particular culture or country? Where do they hang out, or what places do they frequent?

- Develop a tailored approach to immigrants as part of your welcome ministry. Involve immigrant members of your church to brainstorm ideas.

- Be proactive in getting to know the immigrant families in your church. Have someone from the leadership visit their home and spend some time knowing their story and faith journey.

- Be deliberate about promoting diversity within your leadership team.

- Train your leaders on a regular basis on topics that relate to diversity and the role they can play in pursuing unity in the church.

- First impressions matter, and this includes the church website. Does your language sound welcoming and inclusive? Do pictures of your leadership show a diverse group?

- Partner with local branches of offices of World Relief to provide practical resources to help immigrants and refugees.

- Provide ESL classes during the week at the church. Many immigrants coming from non-English countries will appreciate free or low-cost ESL classes in a safe and friendly environment. Learning English helps them feel more comfortable and confident in their interactions with others and plays a major role in their acculturation.

- Not all the foreigners in your neighborhood will show up at your church. Brainstorm creative ways to take church to them. What events can you spearhead and organize in your neighborhood that reach out to immigrants? How can you participate in events organized by them?

- Many of the leading corporations in America have appointed a diversity and inclusion officer to focus on ensuring diversity in their human resources. Churches can take a page from corporate America and maybe appoint someone to be in charge of actively promoting diversity in the church.

APPENDIX 3
Immigrant Heroes of the Bible

The Bible is full of stories of men and women who demonstrated great character in the face of challenge. Many of them share a common characteristic: they were migrants, people on the move, people constantly looking to God for their next step, living with an eternal perspective. Here is a summary of just some of those heroes and their immigrant journeys.

Jacob
Genesis 27–35, 46–50

The grandson of Abraham, Jacob became the second prominent refugee in the Bible after Cain, when he fled for his life after cheating his brother, Esau. He found refuge for twenty years at his uncle Laban's home in Mesopotamia, where he also married Laban's daughters and fathered twelve children.

But his life was far from easy, as he was himself cheated repeatedly by his uncle until he ultimately left to return home to Canaan. Jacob lived in Canaan until, nearly at the end of his life, he moved with his entire family to Egypt where his once-lost son, Joseph, had become the ruler. He died in Egypt, but not before making his sons promise to bury him along with his forefathers in Canaan. It was the land of his birth, but even at the time of his death, his people were still considered foreigners.

Despite Jacob's baggage of lies and deception, God's favor was upon him throughout his life. He was renamed Israel and became the father of the nation that itself would come to be known as *the people without a land.*

Ruth
Ruth 1–4

Ruth was not born a Hebrew but a Moabite. She married into an Israelite family, her parents-in-law having migrated to Moab at the time of a famine. But tragedy struck, and she found herself widowed at a young age. Her Hebrew mother-in-law Naomi, also widowed, chose to return to her hometown, Bethlehem. Ruth insisted on going with Naomi, leaving behind her people and her homeland. She told Naomi, "Where you go I will go, and where you stay I will stay. Your people will be my people and your God my God. Where you die I will die, and there I will be buried" (Ruth 1:16–17).

God honored Ruth's choice. She was found by Boaz, a wealthy Israelite who knew her story. He admired her for how she had left everything and come to live in a strange land, for the sake of her mother-in-law. And he blessed her for seeking refuge with the God of Israel. The two were married, and ultimately became the ancestors of King David as well as Jesus Christ.

Ruth remains in biblical lore as a model of loving-kindness, putting the well-being of others before her own. God used Ruth, a lowly foreigner, to restore Naomi's joy and hope. Her actions were simple, but they cemented her place as a key player in Israel's history.

Esther
Esther 1–10

The book of Esther in the Bible tells the heroic story of a young Jewish orphan woman whose courageous actions helped save her entire people from annihilation. Born as Hadassah and raised by her uncle, Esther is given her new name in the court of King Xerxes when she is crowned queen in place of the previous queen who dared to defy the king's wishes.

In the court of Xerxes, Esther initially does not reveal her Jewish heritage. However, through a series of events this comes to a head. First, she makes the king aware of a plot against him, discovered by her uncle Mordecai. Later, an edict issued by the king under the influence of his wicked advisor, Haman, puts the entire Jewish population across the Persian empire at risk of extermination. Mordecai recognizes God's providence in placing Esther in her position exactly for a time such as this.

Summoning great courage, putting her life and position at risk for a much greater cause, Esther petitions the King, revealing her heritage in the process. Not only are the Jews saved, but Haman is put to death and Mordecai is elevated to the post of Prime Minister. Even to this day, the festival of Purim celebrates God's rescue of the Israelites and the role played by this brave young woman who stepped into her calling in a foreign land.

Nehemiah
Nehemiah 1–13

Nehemiah's story begins more than ninety years after Israel's captivity in Babylon had ended. Nehemiah was a Jewish cupbearer serving the Persian king Artaxerxes I in Susa, more than seven hundred miles from Jerusalem. When he learned that the wall of Jerusalem had still not been rebuilt after its destruction, he was upset. Recalling God's promise to restore the land of the Israelites to them, he was burdened to see that promise fulfilled. With the king's permission and aid, he returned to Jerusalem where, as the governor of Judah, he oversaw the rebuilding of the walls.

He encountered fierce opposition from Israel's enemies who devised multiple schemes to prevent the work from being completed. But God helped Nehemiah foil all of their plots, and it took just fifty-two days for the ambitious rebuilding project to be completed. It was then that he sought to bring reforms to the Jewish community by reviving conformity to the Law of Moses. The book of Nehemiah describes the Jews assembling in prayer and penitence, recalling God's providence, and recommitting themselves to God.

A burden for his homeland had turned into his calling. His eyes were fixed on the home that God had promised His people. And while he trusted God to fulfill His promises, he made it his mission to hold the Jews to their end of the covenant, restoring themselves to an uncompromising commitment to God.

APPENDIX 4

Bible References on Heavenly Rewards

Multitudes who sleep in the dust of the earth will awake: some to everlasting life, others to shame and everlasting contempt. Those who are wise will shine like the brightness of the heavens, and those who lead many to righteousness, like the stars for ever and ever.

Daniel 12:2–3

Blessed are you when people insult you, persecute you and falsely say all kinds of evil against you because of me. Rejoice and be glad, because great is your reward in heaven, for in the same way they persecuted the prophets who were before you.

Matthew 5:11–12

Do not store up for yourselves treasures on earth, where moths and vermin destroy, and where thieves break in and steal. But store up for yourselves treasures in heaven, where moths and vermin do not destroy, and where thieves do not break in and steal. For where your treasure is, there your heart will be also.

Matthew 6:19–21

Whoever welcomes a prophet as a prophet will receive a prophet's reward, and whoever welcomes a righteous person as a righteous person will receive a righteous person's reward. And if anyone gives even a cup of cold water to one of these little ones who is my disciple, truly I tell you, that person will certainly not lose their reward.

Matthew 10:41–42

For the Son of Man is going to come in his Father's glory with his angels, and then he will reward each person according to what they have done.

Matthew 16:27

Jesus answered, "If you want to be perfect, go, sell your possessions and give to the poor, and you will have treasure in heaven. Then come, follow me."

Matthew 19:21

Blessed are you when people hate you, when they exclude you and insult you and reject your name as evil, because of the Son of Man. Rejoice in that day and leap for joy, because great is your reward in heaven. For that is how their ancestors treated the prophets.

Luke 6:22–23

But love your enemies, do good to them, and lend to them without expecting to get anything back. Then your reward will be great, and you will be children of the Most High, because he is kind to the ungrateful and wicked.

Luke 6:35

The one who plants and the one who waters have one purpose, and they will each be rewarded according to their own labor.

1 Corinthians 3:8

For we must all appear before the judgment seat of Christ, so that each of us may receive what is due us for the things done while in the body, whether good or bad.

2 Corinthians 5:10

Slaves, obey your earthly masters with respect and fear, and with sincerity of heart, just as you would obey Christ. Obey them not only to win their favor when their eye is on you, but as slaves of Christ, doing the will of God from your heart. Serve wholeheartedly, as if you were serving the Lord, not people, because you know that the Lord will reward each one for whatever good they do, whether they are slave or free.

Ephesians 6:5–8

Command those who are rich in this present world not to be arrogant nor to put their hope in wealth, which is so uncertain, but to put their hope in God, who richly provides us with everything for our enjoyment. Command them to do good, to be rich in good deeds, and to be generous and willing to share. In this way they will lay up treasure for themselves as a firm foundation for the coming age, so that they may take hold of the life that is truly life.

1 Timothy 6:17–19

I have fought the good fight, I have finished the race, I have kept the faith. Now there is in store for me the crown of righteousness, which the Lord, the righteous Judge, will award to me on that day—and not only to me, but also to all who have longed for his appearing.

2 Timothy 4:7–8

So do not throw away your confidence; it will be richly rewarded. You need to persevere so that when you have done the will of God, you will receive what he has promised.

Hebrews 10:35–36

By faith Moses, when he had grown up, refused to be known as the son of Pharaoh's daughter. He chose to be mistreated along with the people of God rather than to enjoy the fleeting pleasures of sin. He regarded disgrace for the sake of Christ as of greater value than the treasures of Egypt, because he was looking ahead to his reward.

Hebrews 11:24–26

Blessed is the one who perseveres under trial because, having stood the test, that person will receive the crown of life that the Lord has promised to those who love him.

James 1:12

To the elders among you, I appeal as a fellow elder and a witness of Christ's sufferings who also will share in the glory to be revealed: Be shepherds of God's flock that is under your care, watching over them—not because you must, but because you are willing, as God wants you to be; not pursuing dishonest gain, but eager to serve; not lording it over those entrusted to you, but being examples to the flock. And when the Chief Shepherd appears, you will receive the crown of glory that will never fade away.

1 Peter 5:1–4

Look, I am coming soon! My reward is with me, and I will give to each person according to what they have done.

Revelation 22:12

APPENDIX 5
Recommended Reading

On Spiritual Pilgrimage

Motaung, Kate. *A Place to Land: A Story of Longing and Belonging.* Grand Rapids, MI: Discovery House, 2018.

Tozer, A. W. *Culture: Living as Citizens of Heaven on Earth—Collected Insights from A. W. Tozer.* Chicago: Moody Publishers, 2016.

VanLoon, Michelle. *Born to Wander: Recovering the Value of Our Pilgrim Identity.* Chicago: Moody Publishers, 2018.

On Advocating for Immigrants

Gonzalez, Karen. *The God Who Sees: Immigrants, the Bible, and the Journey to Belong.* Harrisonburg, VA: Herald Press, 2019.

Parker, Sarah Rubio. *Far from Home: A Story of Loss, Refuge, and Hope.* Carol Stream, IL: Tyndale Kids, 2019.

Soerens, Matthew, and Jenny Yang. *Welcoming the Stranger: Justice, Compassion & Truth in the Immigration Debate.* Downer's Grove, IL: IVP Books, 2009.

ABOUT THE AUTHOR

Born and raised in Hyderabad, India, Mabel Ninan moved to the US in 2008 shortly after getting married. In thirteen years of marriage, her family has called eleven different places across two continents and seven cities home. The challenges she faced as an immigrant—separation from all things familiar, fracturing of identity, a sense of "homelessness," and the stress of acculturation—led to a spiritual crisis that drew her nearer to God. Realizing that God called her to be an immigrant, she began to draw a parallel between her life as a foreigner and as a believer. The lessons she learned about how to live as a citizen of heaven on earth rekindled her passion for God and inspired her to live boldly for Him.

Mabel's articles have been published in *The Upper Room*, CBN.com, *Leading Hearts Magazine*, and (in)courage.me. She is a contributing writer to Guideposts' *All God's Creatures 2022: Daily Devotions for Animal Lovers*. She won the Shows Great Promise award at the Colorado Christian Writers' Conference in 2018 and the Selah Award for her essay on LeadingHearts.com in 2021.

In India, Mabel was involved in youth ministry from the age of fifteen. In the US, she has volunteered in children's and women's ministries in the many local churches she has called home. She serves as a women's Bible study leader with Bible Study Fellowship in Northern California and is currently pursuing a master's in theological studies from the Southern Baptist Theological Seminary.

A lover of books and tea, Mabel lives with her husband and son in Silicon Valley and blogs on topics that explore the intersection between faith and culture at mabelninan.com.

If you enjoyed this book, will you consider sharing the message with others?

Let us know your thoughts. You can let the author know by visiting or sharing a photo of the cover on our social media pages or leaving a review at a retailer's site. All of it helps us get the message out!

Email: info@ironstreammedia.com

  @ironstreammedia

Brookstone Publishing Group, Iron Stream, Iron Stream Harambee, Iron Stream Fiction, Iron Stream Kids, and Life Bible Study are imprints of Iron Stream Media, which derives its name from Proverbs 27:17, "As iron sharpens iron, so one person sharpens another." This sharpening describes the process of discipleship, one to another. With this in mind, Iron Stream Media provides a variety of solutions for churches, ministry leaders, and nonprofits ranging from in-depth Bible study curriculum and Christian book publishing to custom publishing and consultative services.

For more information on ISM and its imprints, please visit
IronStreamMedia.com